Puzzles
for Programmers and Pros

Dennis E. Shasha

Wiley Publishing, Inc.

Puzzles for Programmers and Pros

Published by
Wiley Publishing, Inc.
10475 Crosspoint Boulevard
Indianapolis, IN 46256
www.wiley.com

Copyright © 2007 by Dennis E. Shasha

Published by Wiley Publishing, Inc., Indianapolis, Indiana

Published simultaneously in Canada

ISBN: 978-0-470-12168-9

Manufactured in the United States of America

10 9 8 7 6 5 4 3 2

Library of Congress Cataloging-in-Publication Data

Shasha, Dennis Elliott.
  Puzzles for programmers and pros / Dennis E. Shasha.
    p. cm.
  Includes index.
  ISBN 978-0-470-12168-9 (paper/website)
  1. Mathematical recreations. 2. Puzzles. I. Title.
  QA95.S4699 2007
  793.74—dc22
                              2007002538

About the Author

Dennis Shasha is a professor of computer science at the Courant Institute of New York University, where he works with biologists on pattern discovery for microarrays, combinatorial design, and network inference; with physicists, musicians, and financial people on algorithms for time series; and on database applications in untrusted environments. Other areas of interest include database tuning as well as tree and graph matching.

Because he likes to type, he has written five books of puzzles before this one, a biography about great computer scientists, and technical books about database tuning, biological pattern recognition, and time series. In addition, he has co-written more than fifty journal papers, sixty conference papers, and seven patents. For fun, he writes the monthly puzzle column for the *Scientific American* website and sometimes for *Dr. Dobb's Journal*.

To omniheurists from every corner of the earth

Credits

Executive Editor
Carol Long

Development Editor
Sara Shlaer

Copy Editor
Mildred Sanchez

Editorial Manager
Mary Beth Wakefield

Production Manager
Tim Tate

Vice President and Executive Group Publisher
Richard Swadley

Vice President and Executive Publisher
Joseph B. Wikert

Graphics and Production Specialists
Brooke Graczyk
Denny Hager
Alicia B. South

Quality Control Technician
Brian H. Walls

Project Coordinator
Kristie Rees

Proofreading
Broccoli Information Management

Indexing
Potomac Indexing, LLC

Anniversary Logo Design
Richard Pacifico

Acknowledgments

My warmest thanks to the readers of my puzzles. They span every continent except Antarctica and they reveal their intelligence with every communication. Some readers have become good friends, such as that gifted teacher and mathematician Andy Liu and the irrepressibly creative architect Mike Whittaker. When a puzzle that I have invented talks back and twists itself into a version that I can't answer, I call in my puzzle brain trust. If I were faced with a math/computational problem of great difficulty, I would huddle with these gifted individuals for a week and we'd solve it.

Many of these puzzles have benefited greatly from the editorial suggestions of *Scientific American's* John Rennie and Jon Erickson and Deirdre Blake of *Dr. Dobb's*. Editors are the first clarity test that an author has of the written version of a puzzle. These editors have surgically exposed any obscurities they have found in my writing. I often pose the oral version of a puzzle to a certain young man named Tyler. Besides solving them (sometimes with the help of a hint or two), he makes it clear when he considers them "lame" (bad) or "ill" (cool). Only the ill ones see print.

Gary Zamchick has graced some of the puzzles with his irreverent cartoons. He has the remarkable ability to capture the essence of a puzzle with just a few pen strokes. This book's Part III, "Faithful Foes," requires Dr. Ecco and you to navigate a labyrinth of tunnels and treachery. Karen Shasha has managed, in her photographs, to portray the spirit of that quest exactly as I have envisioned it.

My acquisitions editor, Carol Long; my development editor, Sara Shlaer; the book's copy editor, Mildred Sanchez; and the book's designer, LeAndra Hosier, have put up with my demands for ever higher visual appeal and supported the demands of the text. If this book is a winner, they are in large part responsible.

Contents

Contents

Contents

Introduction

Some people, like me, love puzzles. Others feel they must study puzzles to succeed at job interviews. I've written this book for both. You'll find here some kick-ass puzzles, but I also take you on a kind of tutorial tour of problem solving techniques to help you face new puzzle challenges. Oh, and then there's the possibility of a prize if you solve the super-hard puzzles at the end.

Puzzles as an interviewing tool have many detractors. Criticism often comes down to the implausibility of a puzzle scenario in which, say, a perfectly logical person is mute and refuses to write. Now, I admit to having written such puzzles, but most of my puzzles come from real problems (e.g., occasionally failing hardware being modeled by occasional liars). In my own research, I try to abstract the problem at hand to a puzzle, in the hopes that I can understand the fundamental issues and take care of the window dressing later. It works pretty well. So, to me, puzzles, especially the right kinds of puzzles, provide a tunnel into scientific and engineering insight.

So why do I write puzzles for other people? First, because they're fun. Second, because they exercise the brain in a useful way. In the puzzle course that Boris talks about in the epigraph, students write programs every week. The programs compete (each having two minutes to run) and the winner gets a Kit Kat bar. I lecture little, offering the techniques you'll find in Part II. By the end of the course, the students find themselves incomparably better at solving the kind of application problems the real world throws at them—problems that algorithms professors will call "intractable" but that nevertheless have to be solved. I can't tell you exactly what brings about the transformation in the students, but it happens.

Most of the puzzles in Part I of this book come from my columns in *Scientific American* and *Dr. Dobb's Journal*, where many readers have given me important and imaginative feedback. That feedback, or sometimes the puzzle itself, has suggested new variants, so you will find more to think about, even if you've already encountered the puzzles in those magazines.

Many times, when I have no idea how to solve a puzzle (and this happens for puzzles I invent, too), I begin with an initial attempt scribbled on paper. It's usually wrong, but sometimes it leads to a better approach. You'll find room to scribble at the end of each puzzle statement in Part I.

Solving puzzles demands a mindset, a vulnerable openness at the beginning followed by a rigorous drive to find a solution—spiritually akin to the technique discussed in Part II called "simulated annealing." Mine is rarely the only possible mindset. When other puzzlists have shared better ideas with me, I present their approaches to you.

Each short chapter in Part I, "Mind Games," presents a puzzle. The solutions to those puzzles appear at the end of Part I. Part II, "The Secret of the Puzzle," shows how to solve several classes of puzzles, both by hand and by computer. You'll find ways to solve elimination puzzles like Sudoku, scheduling puzzles, mathematical word puzzles, and probabilistic puzzles. The approach is unapologetically algorithmic. I believe in using every tool at your disposal. Part III, "Faithful Foes," asks you to solve a mystery involving codes, bank accounts, and geography. You'll accompany a certain mathematical detective named Dr. Ecco and some of his friends. (You may have met them before.) Solve the mystery and you have a chance to win a prize.

Have fun and good luck.

Contest Info

To enter the contest, send your solutions to all the puzzles that appear in Part III to:

    shasha@courant.nyu.edu

The solutions must be submitted in Microsoft Word or PDF format to receive consideration. Entries submitted after August 31, 2008, will not be considered. The author, Dennis E. Shasha, is the sole judge of all entries and will select up to ten entries from among the correct responses. Winners will receive a Wrox T-shirt and baseball cap (or equivalent merchandise), three Wrox books of the winner's choosing, and a Certificate of Omniheurism. To receive the prizes, entrants must supply a street mailing address (no P.O. boxes) along with their entry. Offer void where prohibited by law. Allow six to eight weeks for delivery. Wiley is not responsible for lost, illegible, or incomplete entries. Employees of Wiley Publishing are not eligible to enter.

The cryptograms that appear in Part III of the book are available in Microsoft Word format for download at www.wrox.com. Once at the site, simply use the Search box to locate the book's title or ISBN (978-0-470-12168-9) and click the Download link on the book's detail page to obtain the cryptograms.

p2p.wrox.com

We also invite you to offer variations on any of the puzzles in the book, or alternative solutions, in the P2P forums at p2p.wrox.com. The forums are a Web-based system for you to post messages relating to Wrox books and related technologies and interact with other readers and technology users. The forums offer a subscription feature to e-mail you topics of interest of your choosing when new posts are made to the forums. Wrox authors, editors, other industry experts, and your fellow readers are present on these forums.

At `http://p2p.wrox.com` you will find a number of different forums that will help you not only as you read this book, but also as you develop your own applications. To join the forums, just follow these steps:

1. Go to `p2p.wrox.com` and click the Register link.

2. Read the terms of use and click Agree.

3. Complete the required information to join as well as any optional information you wish to provide and click Submit.

4. You will receive an e-mail with information describing how to verify your account and complete the joining process.

   You can read messages in the forums without joining P2P but in order to post your own messages, you must join.

Once you join, you can post new messages and respond to messages other users post. You can read messages at any time on the Web. If you would like to have new messages from a particular forum e-mailed to you, click the Subscribe to this Forum icon by the forum name in the forum listing.

For more information about how to use the Wrox P2P, be sure to read the P2P FAQs for answers to questions about how the forum software works as well as many common questions specific to P2P and Wrox books. To read the FAQs, click the FAQ link on any P2P page.

Part I
Mind Games

If you can solve these puzzles, you're not management material. You're too good.

 Note: *This Screaming Head icon denotes an especially difficult puzzle.*

COMPETITION

We can't all be winners.

Sweet Tooth

Byzantine Bettors

A Touch of Luck

Information Gain

Reach for the Sky!

Pork Politics

Social Games

Escape Management

Flu Math

Sweet Tooth

Two children, perhaps similar to ones you know, love cake and mathematics. For this reason, Jeremy convinces Marie to play the following game on two identical rectangular cakes chef Martine has prepared for them.

Jeremy will cut the first cake into two pieces, perhaps evenly, perhaps not. After seeing the cut, Marie will decide whether she will choose first or allow Jeremy to do so. If she goes first, she will take the larger piece. If she goes second, she can assume that Jeremy will take the larger piece.

Next, Jeremy will cut the second cake into two pieces (remember that one of the pieces can be vanishingly small if he so chooses). If Marie had chosen first for the first cake, then Jeremy gets to take the larger piece of the second cake. If Marie had chosen second for the first cake, then she gets to take the larger piece of the second cake.

Warm-Up

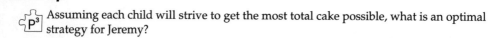 Assuming each child will strive to get the most total cake possible, what is an optimal strategy for Jeremy?

> *Hint: Before you look at the solution: Assume that Jeremy divides the first cake into fractions f and 1-f where f is at least 1/2. Then explore the consequences if Marie chooses to take the piece of fraction f or if she goes second, so gets the piece having fraction 1-f.*

Solution to Warm-Up

Following the hint, Marie reasons as follows: If she takes the fraction f piece, then Jeremy will take the entire second cake (he'll cut the smallest crumb from the second cake and then will take the large first piece, leaving Marie only the crumb). So, Marie will get exactly f and Jeremy will get (1-f) + 1. If Marie takes the smaller piece of the first cake (fraction 1-f), Jeremy will do best if he divides the second cake in half. This gives Marie (1-f) + 1/2. Jeremy follows this reasoning, so realizes that the best he can do is to make f = (1-f) + 1/2. That is 2f = 1 1/2 or f = 3/4. If Marie takes the first piece of the first cake, then Jeremy will get 1/4 of the first cake and all of the second cake. If Marie takes the second piece of the first cake, then Jeremy will get 3/4 of the first cake and 1/2 of the second cake. In both cases, Marie gets a total of 3/4 of a cake and Jeremy 1 1/4. Note that if Jeremy cuts the first cake such that the larger fraction is less than 3/4, Marie will get more than 1/4 of the first cake by going second and will still get 1/2 of the second cake, thus increasing her cake amount beyond 3/4. By contrast, if Jeremy cuts the first cake such that the larger fraction is more than 3/4, Marie will just take that larger piece, again increasing her cake amount beyond 3/4.

I have discussed the warm-up at great length, because a week later a harder challenge has arisen. Chef Martine has made three new identical rectangular cakes. Jeremy and Marie both eye them greedily.

They decide on the following rules. Again, Jeremy will cut. But this time, Marie gets the first choice twice and Jeremy only once. That is, Jeremy cuts the first cake. Marie decides whether she wants to choose first or second for that cake. Next, Jeremy cuts the second cake; again Marie decides whether she wants to choose first or second. Same for the third cake. The only caveat is that Marie must allow Jeremy to choose first at least once.

1. How does Jeremy maximize the amount of cake he gets, given these rules? How much will he get?

2. Suppose there are seven cakes and Marie gets the first choice for six of the seven cakes. Who has the advantage? By how much?

3. Is there any way to ensure that each child receives the same amount of cake, assuming Jeremy always cuts?

Byzantine Bettors

In the popular imagination, Byzantium is famous for the incessant intrigues and plotting that supposedly took place among the courtiers of the palace. Apparently, the Byzantine court in no way deserved this reputation. Modern historical research suggests that Byzantium achieved a remarkable stability and harmony by the standards of the first millennium. Reputations die hard, however, and this puzzle concerns a game show inspired by the imagined intrigues of Byzantium. We call it Byzantine Bettors.

Each bet works as follows. There are some number of "advisors" and you. One advisor will write either 1 or 0 on a piece of paper, show it to the other advisors but not to you, and put that paper face down in front of you. Each advisor will tell you what the value is. They are all very good actors, so no obvious tick or facial expression will reveal to you who is telling the truth. The amount you can wager on each bet is anything from 0 to the total amount you have.

Warm-Up

 Suppose there are four advisors, two of whom always tell the truth, though you don't know which ones. You get three even money bets. You start with $100. How much can you guarantee to win?

Solution to Warm-Up

If all four or three out of four agree on the first bet, then bet the maximum. There must be at least one truth teller in that group. If they are two and two, then bet nothing. After the first bet, you will know who the truth tellers are and will be able to bet the maximum each time. Thus, at least two times you will be able to bet all you have and be sure to win. This will give you a total of $400 at the end.

---

1. Now suppose there are only three advisors and only one of them always tells the truth. Again, you can make three even money bets. You start with $100. How much can you guarantee to win?

The game has just become a little longer but also a lot more nasty. You have four bets, but there is no longer a truth teller, but merely a "partial truth teller." That advisor is not guaranteed to tell the truth all the time, but must do so at least three out of four times. Further, the advisors can actually substitute what's on the paper for a worse result for you once they hear your bet. However, they cannot change the result if so doing would eliminate the possibility that at least one of them is a partial truth-telling advisor.

2. What can you guarantee to win in four bets, with four advisors, three of whom can lie at will, and one who must tell the truth at least three out of four times?

3. Under the reliability conditions of one partial truth teller who tells the truth four out of five times and three liars at will, but assuming you have five bets, can you guarantee to end with at least $150?

A Touch of Luck

The movie *Intacto* posits a world in which luck is a more or less permanent quality of a person. Lucky people are lucky at the gambling table and they are lucky at traffic intersections. But such people have to avoid physical contact with a certain group of people who know how to steal their luck by touch. Finding lucky people is the quest of one of the movie's protagonists. In one case he tests the luck of possible recruits by having them run blindfolded through a forest. The winner is the one who gets to the destination first. Many others crash into one of the trees.

We will try a physically gentler game. In its general form, there are N people and B chances to bet. Every player knows the value of both N and B. Each person starts with an initial (not necessarily equal) wealth in units.

Each bet is an even money bet depending on the flip of a shared fair coin. So, if you bet an amount x and win, your wealth increases by x more. Otherwise you lose the x wagered.

Before each flip, each person bets an amount of his/her choosing (from 0 to any amount he/she has at that point) on either heads or tails.

The winner is the person having the greatest number of units after all B bets are done. If two people tie, then nobody wins. The units are worthless after the betting is done. So, a player receives a reward if and only if he or she is the absolute winner.

Warm-Up

 Bob and Alice have the same number of units and Bob must state his bet first. Suppose there is just one remaining flip of the shared coin. What is Alice's chance of winning?

Solution to Warm-Up

If Bob bets x on heads, then Alice could bet x+1 on heads and Alice will win on heads and will lose on tails. Alternatively, Alice could bet nothing and then Alice will win on tails. Either way, Alice has a probability of 1/2 to win.

Warm-Up 2

 Alice and Bob are the only players again. Alice has more units than Bob. There are five more coin flips to do. If Bob must state his bet before Alice on every flip, then how can Alice maximize her chance to win?

Solution to Warm-Up 2

Alice can win the game every time. For each flip, Alice simply copies Bob's bet. Suppose Bob bets b on heads. Alice bets b on heads too. Whether the shared coin lands on heads or tails, Alice will end up ahead of Bob.

Now here are some challenges for you.

1. Bob, Carol, and Alice play. Alice has 51 units, whereas Bob and Carol have 50 each. Bob must state his bet first, then Carol, and then Alice. Bob and Carol collude to share the reward if either wins. How can Bob and Carol maximize the probability that at least one of them will win if there is just one coin flip left?

2. Does the result change if Alice must state her bet first?

3. Suppose Bob has 51 units, and Alice 50. There are two coin flips left. Bob bets first for the penultimate flip. Alice bets first for the last flip. Does Bob have more than a 1/2 chance of winning? If so, how much more?

4. Suppose Bob has 51 units and Alice 50. Again, there are two coin flips left. This time, Alice bets first for the penultimate flip. Bob bets first for the last flip. Does Bob have more than a 1/2 chance of winning? If so, how much more?

5. Suppose Bob has 51 units and Alice 50. Again, there are two coin flips left. Again, Alice states her bet first in the penultimate round and Bob states his bet first in the final one. This time, Bob announces that he will bet 20 in the penultimate round, though he will wait to see Alice's bet before saying whether he will bet on heads or tails. Can Alice arrange to have more than a 1/2 chance to win?

Like joining a ballet company, winning the Olympics, or getting ahead in a narrow hierarchy of power, the more competition there is for fewer spots, the more risk one must take. Let's see whether you agree.

6. Bob, Alice, Rino, and Juliana have 100 units each and there are two flips left. Each person is out to win—no coalitions. Bob and Alice have bet 100 on heads. Rino has bet 100 on tails. Juliana must now state her bet, knowing that she will state her bet first on the last flip. What are her chances of winning if she bets 90 on either heads or tails? What should she bet?

Information Gain

The well-known and always well-dressed game show host Jeff Nicholas has approached Jordan and his friends Ariana, Bob, Caroline, David, and Ellen with a contest proposition. Jordan and the five are the leading lights of the omniheurist club, a group of outstanding puzzle solvers.

"Our contest is live. I will blindfold your friends, then put a hat on each of them bearing a number between 1 and 10 (more than one person may have the same number) and lead them into a televised game room. Once they have arrived, I will arrange them in a circle in an order that I choose and then replace each blindfold by very dark but non-reflecting sunglasses to eliminate the possibility of eye signals.

"You and the audience will see them in the game room and the numbers on their heads via the television monitor, but they won't be able to see you. I will be holding one blue ticket and one red ticket. You can ask me to deliver one ticket to one of the five. That's all you can do. No knocking on the window or your team will be disqualified.

"The mathematicians may not speak or signal one another in any way, or the entire team will be disqualified. (Obviously, I won't help them in any way other than delivering the ticket.) They will, however, see to whom the ticket is being delivered and the color of the ticket as well as the number on each other person's hat. There is no way they can see the numbers on their own heads.

"At my signal each person will put up a certain number of fingers. If the number of fingers matches the number on that person's hat, then he or she will receive that many thousands of dollars. If all of them win, then you, Jordan, will receive $5,000. If any lose, then you have to buy me a new Armani suit."

"That's it?" Jordan replied. "The only information they receive from the outside is who gets a ticket and the color of that ticket?"

"That's right," said Nicholas. "Remember, though, that each person sees the numbers on the other people's hats too. You may not be able to solve this puzzle. I do want that suit."

1. Is it possible for Jordan to design a protocol to ensure that each of his friends will raise the correct number of fingers? If so, explain it. If not, does Jordan have a high probability of winning?

Warm-Up

Here's a much easier problem to give you an idea of the kind of protocol Jordan might design. Suppose Jeff Nicholas were required to put consecutive numbers on the five hats (as in 4, 5, 6, 7, 8). Then what could Jordan do?

Solution to Warm-Up

Jordan could arrange the following protocol with his friends. Let Ariana represent 1, Bob represent 2, Caroline represent 3, David represent 4 and Ellen represent 5 and 6. If Jordan sends a ticket to Ariana, then the consecutive numbers start with 1. If to Bob, then they start with 2. If to Caroline, then 3. If to David, then 4. If a blue ticket to Ellen, then 5. If a red ticket to Ellen, then 6.

Thus, when Jordan sends in a ticket, each mathematician will know the first number in the sequence. And by looking at the numbers on his or her fellow players' hats, that mathematician can work out by process of elimination which number appears on his or her own hat.

In the Jeff Nicholas challenge, however, the numbers are not necessarily consecutive or even all distinct. Do you think it can be done?

Reach for the Sky!

Reach for the Sky! is based on hollow lottery balls. Here is how it is played.

Your adversary is given 100 identical pieces of paper. In a room hidden from your view, he writes a number on each one—he can choose any value in the range 1 to 1 million but without duplicates—then inserts them into small opaque envelopes. Subsequently, these papers are given to an independent third party called the "stuffer." The stuffer works in full view of you and your adversary at all times. He shows you 100 hollow and empty lottery balls. He then shuffles the envelopes and inserts one envelope into the first lottery ball, another into the second, and so on up to 100. After inserting each envelope, he screws the ball shut. These balls have been examined using drop tests, bounce tests, and resiliometric tests to be sure they all share the same physical properties.

The stuffer then puts the balls into a lottery machine. The lottery machine mixes the balls thoroughly until one comes out. Call that ball number 1. The ball is opened and you are told the value on the paper (what we will call the 'paper value' for short). You have the option to 'capture' that paper value or not. If you capture it, you put it in your capture pile and you have used up one capture. If you don't, it goes in the discard pile never to come out, though you may find it useful to remember the discarded paper values. Repeat this procedure for all 100 balls. You are allowed three 'captures' altogether. Your goal is to capture the highest paper value written by your adversary. If you do, you win $100,000. If you don't, you lose $100,000. Should you engage in this bet? If so, what is your probability of winning?

This puzzle is a variant on the sultan's daughters problem. A young suitor may choose any of the 100 daughters of the sultan. They are presented to him in some random order. He has little basis for judgment, so judges only by outward beauty and grace. If he rejects one, he never sees her again. Once he selects one, he must marry her and no other.

Warm-Up

 Can you design a strategy that gives the suitor at least a 1/4 chance of marrying the most beautiful daughter, assuming the daughters are presented to him in an order that is unlikely to be related to their beauty, e.g., based on the hour and minute of the day in which they were born?

Solution to Warm-Up

Look at but reject the first half of the daughters. Then take the first daughter who is more beautiful than any of those you have seen so far. This does not guarantee that you will marry the most beautiful daughter (or any daughter at all), but it has the virtue of offering an easy rough analysis: you have a 1/2 chance that the most beautiful daughter is in the second half and a 1/2 chance that the second most beautiful daughter is in the first half. The two together arise with probability 1/4, assuming the daughters are presented to you in an order that is independent of their beauty—a situation that likely holds in the hour-minute ordering mentioned above. That case is sufficient to ensure that you marry the most beautiful daughter. In fact, other cases also lead to this outcome. For example, the third most beautiful daughter could be in the first half and the most beautiful one could precede the second most beautiful one in the second half. A deeper analysis shows that it is better, in fact, to reject the first 37 daughters and then choose the next one that is more beautiful than any you have seen.

1. What would be a good strategy for the $100,000 Reach for the Sky! game, where you have three captures? Using that strategy, what would be your chance of winning?

   Hint: A bit of programming might come in handy.

2. How would your answer change if there were 1,000 lottery balls?

Pork Politics

A grant of a whopping 100 million dollars is available to the five districts making up a state. The districts have representation proportional to their population in the state assembly. District A has 35 representatives, district B has 25, district C has 16, district D has 14, and district E has 10.

If a coalition consisting of at least 51 members forms, then they can force the funds to come to their districts, where the money will be divided proportionally to the representation. For example, if the districts having 35 and 25 get together, they can force all 100 million to go to their two districts and that money will be divided such that $(35/60) \times 100$ million goes to the district A and $(25/60) \times 100$ million goes to B. Each district has only its own self-interest in mind.

Warm-Up

 What would B most prefer?

Solution to Warm-Up

B prefers the coalition {B, C, E} to any other winning coalition, because B would get the fraction 25/55 of the money, whereas if B allied itself with A, it would get only 25/60 of the money.

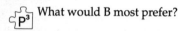

1. Which coalitions might form?

The representatives of B have an ancient privilege. They can control the rules of when an allocation can take place. That is, they may require that an allocation require only a simple majority as we've assumed until now, but they can also demand that it require a 67% majority, or a 75% majority.

2. How strong a majority should B prefer (51%, 67%, or 75%) in order for B to receive as much money as possible?

Social Games

Since Adam Smith observed that the "invisible hand" of the free market would force self-interested manufacturers to offer low prices to consumers, governments and politics have never been the same. It took almost two more centuries, however, to achieve a proper mathematical analysis of the consequences of selfish behavior beginning with Morgenstern's and Von Neumann's game theory and the work of John Nash. (You may recall Nash as the mathematician who was the subject of the movie *A Beautiful Mind*.)

This puzzle explores game theory as it applies to social goods. Let's start with the invisible hand.

Bob and Alice are competitive manufacturers. If they fix their prices at a high level, then they will share the market and each will receive a profit of 3. If Alice decides to lower prices while Bob doesn't, then Alice will enjoy a profit of 4 while Bob gets a profit of 0, because nobody will buy from him. At that point, Bob will lower his price to receive at least a profit of 1. Similarly, Bob receives 4 and Alice 0 if the roles are reversed. Simply following their self-interest, both will lower their prices and their profits will drop to 1 each.

This arrangement can be expressed in the following table, where Bob's profit is shown on the left in each pair and Alice's profit is on the right. So, the upper right corner, for example, represents the state in which Bob charges a high price (and receives a profit of 0) and Alice charges a low price (and receives a profit of 4).

	Alice High	Alice Low
Bob High	3, 3	0, 4
Bob Low	4, 0	1, 1

John Nash defined the concept of an *equilibrium state*, since known as a *Nash equilibrium*, in which no party has an interest in deviating from that state. The only Nash equilibrium in this case is the bottom right corner. Neither Bob nor Alice will unilaterally raise prices. If Bob raised prices (thus moving the state to the upper right corner), then his profit would decrease to 0. If Alice raised prices, she would move to the lower left corner, thus decreasing her profits to 0.

This is the invisible hand at work. For the consumers, Bob and Alice's competition leads to lower prices, a social good. Virtually every modern economy gives evidence of this.

Unfortunately, selfishness does not always lead to socially beneficial consequences. Suppose that instead of representing price choices of competitive manufacturers, the table represented choices about honesty or social responsibility. That is, the "High" row represents states in which Bob acts honestly. By contrast, the "Low" row represents a situation in which Bob cheats (say, steals, pollutes, or bribes lawmakers). The upper right corner portrays a state in which Alice cheats but Bob doesn't. As you can see, the cheater then benefits. If both cheat, then their benefits go down. Selfishness leads to social loss. Corrupt nations, high crime zones, and brawling families give much evidence of this.

Game theory is neutral. The same game matrix and the same Nash equilibrium can lead to a good or bad state. Selfishness can yield a social benefit or harm.

Now, let us say that it is your job to design public policy. You are confronted with the matrix representing the selfish benefits of cheating and you want to change it somehow. So you establish a police force and criminal justice system that makes it 10 percent likely that cheaters will be caught and given a value of -5 (e.g., jail time).

In that case, Alice's benefit in the upper right corner has a 90 percent probability of being 4 and a 10 percent probability of being -5. Thus, her expected benefit is $(4 \times 0.9) + ((-5) \times 0.1)$ or 3.1. In terms of expectations, the matrix becomes:

	Alice Honest	Alice Cheats
Bob Honest	3, 3	0, 3.1
Bob Cheats	3.1, 0	0.4, 0.4

Now, the benefits of cheating when starting from the honest-honest state are much reduced. Further, if the punishment increases or the probability of being caught increases, then honest-honest may become a Nash equilibrium.

Warm-Up

 Suppose you can increase punishments (i.e., make them more negative). Can you do so in a way to make the upper left a Nash equilibrium while keeping the bottom right a Nash equilibrium as well? Assume you cannot change the probability of being caught.

Solution to Warm-Up

Suppose the punishment becomes -8. Alice's gain in the upper right corner state becomes $(4 \times 0.9) + ((-8) \times 0.1) = 2.8$. The gains at the bottom right become $(1 \times 0.9) + ((-8) \times 0.1) = 0.1$. This yields the matrix:

	Alice Honest	Alice Cheats
Bob Honest	3, 3	0, 2.8
Bob Cheats	2.8, 0	0.1, 0.1

So, honest-honest is a Nash equilibrium, because neither Bob nor Alice has an incentive to cheat to leave this state. On the other hand, the lower right hand corner is also a Nash equilibrium. If both Bob and Alice cheat, then they each still receive a tiny expected gain. If one then becomes honest, that person's gain is eliminated.

Here are some challenges for you.

1. How would punishment have to change to eliminate cheats-cheats as a Nash equilibrium?

As civilizations have advanced, societies have evolved the notion of punishments that fit the crime. This principle might limit the extent to which overly severe punishments are considered acceptable.

2. If you are a public policy maker and you want to limit the punishment for cheating to -5, how much must you increase the probability of catching criminals to maintain the upper left as the only Nash equilibrium?

In modern societies, inequalities exist so that the benefits of an honest society may benefit one party more than another. Say that Bob gets 5 whereas Alice gets only 2 if both are honest. Assuming for the moment that the probability of being caught is 0, this gives us the following game matrix:

	Alice Honest	**Alice Cheats**
Bob Honest	5, 2	0, 4
Bob Cheats	4, 0	1, 1

The total social good of the upper left corner has increased at the cost of inequality. One side effect, however, is that incentives to dishonesty now change.

3. Assuming a 10 percent likelihood of being caught, is there a punishment value that would cause the only Nash equilibrium to be the upper right state (Alice commits crime but Bob does not)?

4. Still assuming a 10 percent likelihood of being caught, what must the punishment be to force Alice to stay honest?

Let's close this puzzle on a non-punishment note. Let's return, in fact, to the competing manufacturers Bob and Alice. Recall their game matrix.

	Alice High	**Alice Low**
Bob High	3, 3	0, 4
Bob Low	4, 0	1, 1

The invisible hand guides them to lower prices, but neither likes this. They see that if they cooperated, their total profit would be $3 + 3 = 6$ instead of $1 + 1 = 2$ as in the competing scenario. For that reason, they might consider merging their two enterprises into BobAlice and thereby achieving a total profit of 6 instead of 2. That is, when Bob looks at Alice, he doesn't value her company at the profit of 1 that she is currently achieving, but at a profit of 5, the additional profit she could bring to a potential BobAlice relative to Bob in a competing world. Of course, this increased profit to Bob and Alice comes at an approximately equal cost to the consumer.

Next time you hear someone expound about inequality, crime, enlightened self-interest, and antitrust laws, bring out your game matrices. You may find more wisdom in them than in the blah-blah.

Escape Management

A thief has just robbed a bank at the center of a city. He has done the robbery quietly, so he believes he is not being tracked. In fact, though, a silent alarm has alerted the police to the theft and they know the exact position of the thief. Their hope is to catch the thief and his accomplices.

The city is laid out as a 19×19 road grid. The thief (T) starts exactly in the center, that is, nine blocks from any border. Figure 1-1 shows the upper right portion of the whole grid. The thief begins to drive north towards the first intersection in the northern half of the city. At every intersection the car can go right, left, or straight (not backwards). The thief will escape if he arrives at either the northern or southern edges.

The police (P) want to let the thief move to see where T will go with his car, but they want to prevent the car from leaving the grid, at least for a while.

At every intersection, the thief chooses where to go except that the police, by their presence, can force T to go straight or to turn right or left. On the other hand, the police want to leave T as much freedom as possible. They therefore have to decide how to deploy their resources to achieve one of several outcomes.

1. The police want to control T's direction at only five intersections. They know that T is extremely motivated to escape. How long (in terms of single block steps) at most will it take T to arrive at either the northern or southern border?

2. Suppose that the police want to prevent T from reaching the northern or southern borders. Therefore the police plan to control T's direction m out of every n times for some m < n. What should m and n be to minimize the fraction of time P forces T to change directions while still preventing T from escaping?

Figure 1-1: The thief T starts where indicated. He is nine blocks from the northern, eastern, southern, and western borders, though only the first two are shown.

3. How does your answer change if T can escape by reaching any border, including the eastern and western ones?

Flu Math

Suppose the government health authorities tell you that you have a 5% chance of dying from a flu vaccine but a 10% chance of contracting and dying of the flu when an epidemic strikes if you don't take the vaccine. Do you take the vaccine assuming it offers perfect protection?

Many people refuse.

This apparent irrationality is commonly attributed to "omission bias" — people tend to prefer inaction to action. But I think there are other reasons. For one thing, the authorities commonly have a bias towards action — if only to justify their own existence. If so, the consequences of the flu may be overstated or the risks of the vaccine may be understated.

But even if these probabilities are to be believed and the bias towards inaction is corrected, there is the observation that the risk of being unvaccinated decreases if most other people take the flu vaccine.

Suppose, in fact, that your likelihood of dying from the flu when unvaccinated goes down according to the following formula: If a fraction f (excluding you) of people take the flu shot, then your probability of dying from the flu is just $(1-f) \times 10\%$. For example, if 65% of the people take it and you are among the 35% who do not, then the probability of your contracting the flu is $0.35 \times 10\% = 3.5\%$.

Warm-Up

Suppose a government official could require 60% of the people to take the vaccine. Then what would be the average risk of death for the entire population due to the flu?

Solution to Warm-Up

Recall that if the official doesn't allow anyone to take the vaccine, then the death toll is 10%. If the official forces everyone to take it, the death toll is 5%. If 60% take the shot, then those people have a 5% chance of dying, but the others have only a 40% chance of dying from the flu, so the death toll among them is 4%. The overall death toll, therefore, is $(0.6 \times 5\%) + (0.4 \times 4\%) = 4.6\%$.

---

1. As long as the government is in a compelling mode, what fraction should be required to take the vaccine in order to minimize the overall average risk?

On the other hand, suppose that the government feels it cannot (or, preferably, should not) compel people to take the vaccine. Instead, the government offers each person the flu shot in turn. If a person refuses, then there is no second chance. Each person knows how many people took the flu shot among those already offered. Each person believes and knows that everyone else believes the government's risk figures (5% if a person takes it; 10% modified by the f formula above if a person doesn't). Each person will take the flu shot if and only if it helps him or her. There is no regard for the greater good.

2. Under these conditions (no compulsion, full belief in government risk figures, self-ishness), what percentage of people will take the flu shot?

3. Suppose 25% of the population will not take the vaccine under any circumstances. Nobody else knows beforehand who they are. Then can you determine what percentage of people will in fact take the vaccine under the same assumptions?

The government looks at these results and decides that a little benevolent disinformation is in order. That is, the government will inflate the risk of disease to a number R greater than 10% but with the risk of contracting the flu if one is unvaccinated decreasing based on the f formula, with the 10% replaced by R—that is, $(1-f) \times R$. The exaggerated risk strategy is a carefully guarded secret, so everyone believes the government and knows that everyone else does too.

4. Again, the government will compel nobody. To which percentage should the risk of disease be inflated to achieve the vaccination level you determined in your answer to question 1?

Disclaimer: The actual death rates from the flu and flu vaccines are typically far smaller than the numbers used in these examples. Also, the scenario of benevolent disinformation is purely invented. Purely.

DESIGN

Imagination rules...

Whipping Ice

Optimal Jargon

Using Your Marbles

Flipping Colors

Scheduling Tradition

Fractal Biology

As Easy as Pie

Whipping Ice

Remember Indiana Jones and his bullwhip? In these problems, Indy must overcome a series of obstacles to reach his goal. Indy stands on a board resembling a skateboard but that cannot tilt. Under the chassis are four metal ball bearings on universal swivels. He travels over a smooth frozen lake that has narrow wooden poles sticking up and out of the ice.

Here are the rules:

i. If he is going in a given direction and has not wrapped the whip around any pole, then he will keep going in a straight line. He cannot otherwise force the chassis to turn.

ii. The whip is light, so throwing it in any direction does not change his direction materially.

iii. He can unwhip a whip from a pole at will.

iv. He can pull on the whip or just let it rotate him, but pushing the whip has no effect.

Warm-Up

In Figure 1-2, you see a challenge for Indy to get from one end of a corridor that is partly blocked by two barriers to the other end. Assuming Indy can approach the corridor at any angle, how can he reach the other end without touching any barriers?

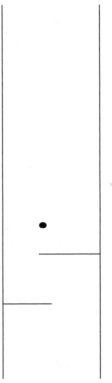

Figure 1-2: How can Indy use his whip to navigate from the bottom of the corridor to the top without hitting the barriers or the sides? Assume he can approach the bottom from any angle. The dot represents a pole.

Solution to Warm-Up

Figure 1-3 shows a solution. Indy comes in at an angle and then throws the whip as indicated by the dashed line to rotate around the pole.

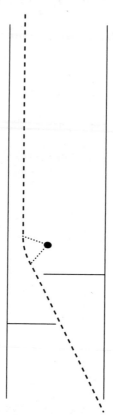

Figure 1-3: Indy connects briefly to the pole (the dark circle) to rotate to a line parallel to the walls of the corridor.

Now here are the two problems for you:

1.   Does Indy need more poles than the two shown by the dark circles in Figure 1-4 to go from the bottom to the top?

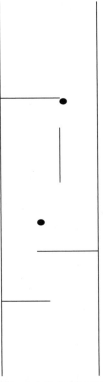

Figure 1-4: Indy wants to go from the bottom to the top without hitting the barriers or the walls. Indy may enter the bottom at any angle. Can Indy do it with the two poles indicated as black circles?

2. There are several L-shaped barriers and several objects (at the Xs in Figure 1-5) that Indy wants to collect in a game called Treasure Skater. What is the minimum number of poles he will need and where should he place them?

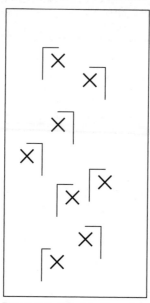

Figure 1-5: What is the minimum number of poles Indy will need to skate over all the Xs?

Optimal Jargon

Everywhere you look, you find mini-fads and their accompanying industries. Each comes with a bunch of characteristic phrases that often yield to a kind of popular jargon. To send a text message to someone becomes "to text them." To find information using the Google search engine becomes "to google it." Such shortening of phrases is not unique to our time. Movie sets shorten the phrase "we are about to start cameras so actors prepare yourselves and everyone else be quiet" to the single word "camera." Languages borrow jargon from one another, because of the economy of expression they offer. Even linguistically proud France borrows "milestone" and "IP" from English, whereas it would never think of borrowing, say, "spoon."

As puzzlists, we can help make better jargon. To show you how, we'll abstract the phrases into letters and find an encoding in terms of bits. The marketeers can find words to fit later. We'll be very concrete to avoid having to estimate probabilities.

Suppose that every message communicated has 60 characters and each character is one of A, B, C, or D. If you have to encode these in bits and you know nothing else, you might encode them as follows:

```
A - 00
B - 01
C - 10
D - 11
```

Because there are 60 characters and each character is encoded in two bits, the whole message requires 120 bits (15 bytes). Whereas this yields a far more succinct expression than the one byte per character encoding of ASCII, for example, some more information might improve things still further.

Warm-Up

Suppose that we knew that every message of 60 characters consisted of exactly 30 As, 15 Bs, 10 Cs, and 5 Ds. What would be a good encoding in bits of the characters then?

Solution to Warm-Up

Intuition tells us that a good encoding should render A in the fewest bits, then B, then C, and then D. It is that intuition that guided Samuel Morse in his invention of the code that bears his name. But Information Theory could conceivably help us do better.

As originally conceived by Claude Shannon, Information Theory was closely inspired by a statistical mechanics interpretation of thermodynamics. Shannon defined a notion of "entropy" as a formula involving the probability of each character (e.g., A has probability $30/60$ or $1/2$; whereas D has probability $5/60$ or $1/12$), and logs of probabilities. The entropy describes the weighted average length of an optimal encoding in bits of a single character. The entropy formula in this case yields: $(1/2 \log(2)) + (1/4 \log(4)) + (1/6 \log(6)) + (1/12 \log(12))$ where all the logs are to the base 2. This comes out to about 1.73 bits per character. Of course, a designer is free to choose the encoding he or she wishes, and we choose a whole number of bits for each character, as follows:

```
A-1
B-01
C-000
D-001
```

In our encoding, sending A thirty times would cost 30, sending B 15 times would cost 30 as well, and so on. The total length would be $30 + (15 \times 2) + (10 \times 3) + (5 \times 3) = 105$ bits. This comes out to 105/60 or 1.75 bits per character. So the intuitive design is quite good.

So far, we've considered only the single character frequencies. We may in fact know more. For example, in English, "q" is rare and so is "u," but "u" almost always follows "q." So we might consider encoding "qu" as a single character. Could this help us?

1. Suppose that in addition to the frequencies given in the warm-up, you know that in every message B is always followed by A and D is always followed by C. Could you arrive at a shorter encoding of the message?

To be really useful, jargon must reduce long phrases to a word or two. So, let's see if we can simulate that case.

2. Suppose that in addition to the frequencies given in the warm-up, you know that in every message, D is always followed by C, C is always followed by B, and B is always followed by A. Could you arrive at an even shorter encoding of a 60-character message? Which phrases should be rendered as jargon?

English is famous for its exceptions to almost all rules (e.g., the country "Iraq" has a "q" that is not followed by a "u"). Such exceptions could force an optimal encoding to include a codeword for "q" as well as one for "qu." But if there were many exceptions, then the extra codewords might not be worth it. Let's see how this plays out in our mini-language.

3. Suppose that in addition to the frequencies given in the warm-up, you know that in every message, D is always followed by C, C is always followed by B, and B is followed by A 13 out of 15 times? What is the shortest encoding you could find of a 60-character message?

Using Your Marbles

Your friend Carol loves to prepare gifts of marbles in bags for children. On Monday, she has 5 red marbles, 6 blue marbles, and 7 white ones.

Warm-Up

 How many different bags can she pack so each bag will have a different collection of marbles? Two bags are different if for at least one color, one bag has a different number of marbles of that color from the other. For example, a bag with two red marbles and one blue is different from a bag having one red and one blue or a bag having one red and two blue.

Solution to Warm-Up

For brevity, the colors will be represented by their first letters: R (red), B (blue), and W (white). Carol can pack ten different bags: R, B, W, RR, BB, WW, RB, BW, RW, BWW.

That was just the warm-up.

1. On Tuesday, she again starts with 5 red marbles, 6 blue marbles, and 7 white ones. In order to make the bags more varied, she wants to pack the bags so that each bag differs by at least two "in-or-outs" from any other bag. An in-or-out consists of inserting a marble into a bag or removing a marble from a bag. So, for example, R and RR differ by only one in-or-out (insert R). On the other hand, RW and RB differ by two (remove W and insert B). How many different bags of marbles can Carol create that differ by at least two in-or-outs?

On Wednesday, Carol is given a bag that she cannot open.

2. She knows she has 18 marbles. She also knows that there is at least one red, at least one blue, and at least one white. Knowing only this information, but before seeing the marbles, Carol receives a phone call. "Can you guarantee to be able to give each child a bag with a different collection of marbles (i.e., at least one in-or-out apart), if there are eight children at a party? If not, then can you make this guarantee if there are seven children? If so, then how about nine?" How should Carol answer?

3. On Thursday, she again knows only that she has 18 marbles and at least one of each color, and is in the same situation as Tuesday as far as wanting the children to enjoy variety. So she wants each gift to differ from every other by at least two in-or-outs. How many children can she guarantee to prepare bags for in that case?

4. On Friday, her friend Diane packs the bags. Diane assures Carol that (i) every bag contains a different (some difference of number in at least one color) collection of marbles, (ii) that there are 18 marbles to start with, (iii) there are more white than blue and more blue than red, and (iv) that the maximum different ones she could pack was seven. Assuming that Diane is an extremely capable packer, what is the maximum number of red marbles there could have been at the beginning?

Flipping Colors

The well-known knight's tour problem is the challenge of placing a knight at a starting position on a chessboard and having it visit every square on the board exactly once. You can look up the knight's tour problem on the Web to get inspiration for the much harder puzzle I'm going to ask you to do. In fact, you may decide this problem is not even possible.

This puzzle also concerns a knight, but we are going to suppose that each knight move consists of traveling two squares vertically and one square horizontally or two horizontally and then one vertically. Each move of the knight flips the colors of the three squares along the L-shaped path chosen, (not including the starting square, but including the landing square). The problem is to place the knight at an initial square of your choice, then move the knight through a series of L-shaped moves in such a way that the color of each square on the board is the reverse of the color before the knight began its journey. Assume that when you place the knight on a square to start, you flip the color of that square first.

Note that the knight may flip the color of a square more than once but must ultimately flip it an odd number of times.

1. Can the knight flip the color of every square an odd number of times? If so, in how few moves?

Scheduling Tradition

There are 12 school teams, unimaginatively named A, B, C, D, E, F, G, H, I, J, K, and L. They must play one another on 11 consecutive days on six fields. Every team must play every other team exactly once. Each team plays one game per day.

Warm-Up

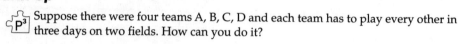

Suppose there were four teams A, B, C, D and each team has to play every other in three days on two fields. How can you do it?

Solution to Warm-Up

We'll represent the solution in two columns corresponding to the two playing fields. Thus, in the first day, A plays B on field 1 and C plays D on field 2.

```
AB  CD
AC  DB
AD  BC
```

Not only does the real problem involve 12 teams instead of merely four, but there are certain constraints due to traditional team rivalries: A must play B on day 1, G on day 3, and H on day 6. F must play I on day 2 and J on day 5. K must play H on day 9 and E on day 11. L must play E on day 8 and B on day 9. H must play I on day 10 and L on day 11. There are no constraints on C or D because these are new teams.

1. Can you form an 11-day schedule for these teams that satisfies the constraints?

It may seem difficult, but look again at the warm-up. Look in particular at the non-A columns. They are related to one another. If you understand how, you can solve the harder problem.

Fractal Biology

Biologists study not only genes, but also genomes, proteomes, interactomes, basically anything *omic*, that is, anything having to do with entire species. It's a perspective that might hurt many delicate human egos.

For example, we have roughly the same number of genes as mice and most are very similar in form and function. We think of ourselves as a higher form of life, but the genome itself doesn't bear that out. The difference must be in the interactions, the networks of binding and repulsion that give rise to the unique capabilities of each species.

A puzzle that obsesses biologists is to figure out why protein interaction networks have the topologies they do. You see, most proteins have very few connections, and very few have many connections. We call members of the latter groups the *hubs*. This gives rise to what are sometimes called *scale-free* networks reminiscent of Mandelbrot's fractals or in fact the Web. You can build a scale-free network as follows: Make 70 percent of all nodes have one edge and the remaining 30 percent have two or more. Of the 30 percent, 70 percent have two edges exactly and 30 percent have three edges or more. Of these 30 percent, 70 percent have three edges exactly and 30 percent have four edges or more, and so on.

One theory is that scale-free networks have good failure properties. The thinking goes like this: Because mutations strike randomly at the genome, most mutations will wound proteins that interact with very few other proteins, thus are presumably less important. Fatal mutations of hub proteins can occur too, but they are rare, because hubs are rare.

A typical problem is to determine how many interaction links are needed to achieve high fault tolerance while ensuring that no unwounded protein is more than two interaction links away from another one.

If there were just four protein nodes, then a simple square of interactions would achieve this goal (see Figure 1-6). Removing any node allows any remaining pair of nodes to communicate over at most two links.

Figure 1-6: A four-node network in which there is a one- or two-link path from any node to any other even if a node is deleted.

Warm-Up

 Can you achieve this distance two condition for six nodes even if one node is wounded (call that the *wounded distance two condition*), using ten links or fewer and assuming no node can have more than three interaction links?

Solution to Warm-up

Figure 1-7 shows a nine-link solution.

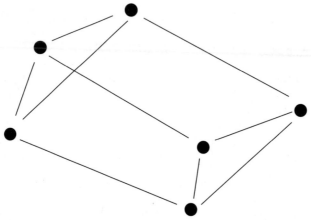

Figure 1-7: A six-node network in which there is a one- or two-link path from any node to any other even if a node is deleted.

---

1. Can you achieve the wounded distance two condition for eight nodes using 16 links, assuming no node can have more than four interaction links?

2. What is the fewest number of links needed to achieve the wounded distance two condition for twelve nodes and at most five interaction links for any node?

3. What is the fewest number of links needed for 12 nodes, but without any limit on the number of interaction links any particular node can have?

4. We have a particular network having 108 proteins. We don't yet know all the interactions. What is the fewest number of links needed to achieve the wounded distance two condition for any pair among these 108 nodes if there is a limit of 60 interactions that any single node can have? Try for a solution that uses fewer than 600 links.

P^3

As Easy as Pie

If you've ever asked a young child to cut a pie for several people, the child will likely cut a piece for himself or herself and then pass you the knife. Perpendicular cuts across the length of the pie come naturally to adults for the sake of overall efficiency. Young children simply find this to be too altruistic. This puzzle is an attempt to help you recapture that inner child.

You will design a series of cuts to partition a square pie into equal pieces to share among several people. The piece finally offered to each person is called a "final piece." Here are the rules:

i. All cuts must be straight, vertical, and parallel to one of the original sides.

ii. All final pieces must contain the same amount of pie volume (and, because of the first rule) the same amount of the top of the pie.

iii. (Child cut rule) Every cut should yield one final piece except the last one, which yields two final pieces.

The goal, which admittedly might occur only to a lazy, clever, or lazy and clever child, is to minimize the sum of the perimeters of all the final pieces.

Warm-Up

 We start with the square pie in Figure 1-8.

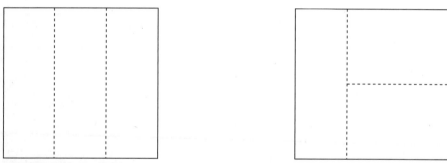

Figure 1-8: Two possible ways of cutting the original pie (above) into three pieces of equal size. The bottom left shows two parallel cuts. The bottom right shows two perpendicular cuts.

We could cut that square pie using two parallel cuts (A) or using two perpendicular cuts. Both satisfy the three rules: equal size final pieces, vertical cuts, and child cut rule. Which yields a smaller total perimeter?

Solution to Warm-Up

In the parallel cut case (A), each final piece has a perimeter of length $1 + 1/3 + 1 + 1/3 = 8/3$. So the three final pieces altogether have a total perimeter of 8. Two perpendicular cuts (B) yield a first final piece having perimeter 8/3 and the remaining two final pieces each having perimeter: $2/3 + 1/2 + 2/3 + 1/2 = 7/3$. In this case, the total perimeter is 7 1/3.

Now it's your turn.

1. Find a cut design obeying the above three rules that minimizes the total length of the perimeters for five pieces.

For the remaining questions, let's pretend we're working with adults. So, we drop the child cut rule, but keep the first two.

2. How much better can you do for five pieces, after dropping the child cut rule?

3. What about nine pieces?

   Hint: There is a Russian doll feeling about this one.

4. Can you get a smaller perimeter for five pieces, if, in addition to dropping the child cut rule, you drop the rule that cuts must be parallel to the original sides?

Try this puzzle on a smart child sometime. Enjoy the reaction you get. In my experience, someone always ends up laughing.

CHANCE

Getting on the right side of luck

Lucky Roulette

Legal Logic

The Box Chip Game

Feedback Dividends

Lucky Roulette

Interviews at hi-tech companies often include puzzles. Here is one that has made the rounds in spite of its violent setting. We will spice it up a bit.

I put two bullets in two adjacent chambers of a six shot revolver. I point it at your head and pull the trigger. Click. You are still alive. The chamber has advanced by one. I am prepared to try again.

Warm-Up

 Is it better for you if I spin again or not before pulling the trigger a second time?

Solution to Warm-Up

It's better for you to keep the chamber where it is, i.e., not to spin. Why? Well, let E represent an empty chamber and B represent a chamber with a bullet.

Putting the chamber first used at the beginning on the left, the gun could have been in any of the following configurations with equal probability:

```
BBEEEE
EBBEEE
EEBBEE
EEEBBE
EEEEBB
BEEEEB
```

Because you didn't die, the equi-probable configurations left are:

```
EBBEEE
EEBBEE
EEEBBE
EEEEBB
```

If I don't spin, then you die in only 1 in 4 cases on the second trigger pull. If I spin, you have a 1 out of 3 chance to die. So, you don't want me to spin.

Now suppose I am going to pull the trigger two more times for a total of four. If you survive the second trigger pull, then you must be in one of these cases:

```
EEBBEE
EEEBBE
EEEEBB
```

1.   Do you ask for a spin of the chamber before the third trigger pull? How about before the fourth trigger pull? Using your best strategy, what are your chances of survival given that you've survived the first trigger pull?

Legal Logic

In my last year of college, I briefly flirted with the idea of going to law school. The reasoning seemed kind of fun. Lots of people (some might say too many) were doing it. But I chose technology, deciding that for the most part lawyers divide an existing wealth pie and take a slice for themselves: a zero sum game for society. A career in technology promised the possibility of increasing the size of the pie. Of course, my analysis was simplistic, but I still think fundamentally correct. Technology opens new worlds. Legal reasoning retreads paths that the Mesopotamians blazed more than 4,000 years ago. Still, my career has since brought me in close contact with very smart lawyers. I have seen how they argue and how their arguments affect society. I offer you a small axiomatization of what I think is going on and then propose a modest reform.

Suppose there is a new device (or drug) D aimed at sickness S. Legal logic plays with the following predicates:

> `mayuse(x,D)` — Person x may use device D (i.e., D is available).
>
> `hurtby(x, D)` — Person x has been hurt by device D.
>
> `newdevice(D)` — Device D is new.
>
> `sick(x,S)` — Person x is sick with sickness S.
>
> `sueandwin(x)` — Person x sues someone with a good probability of winning.

This is first order predicate logic so:

> `"ThereExists x such that ..."` means at least one person x has the property represented by the ellipses.
>
> `"ForAll x ..."` means that all people have the property represented by the ellipses.
>
> A→B means that if A holds, then B must hold. If A doesn't hold, then B need not either.

❑   Rule 1) `ForAll x hurtby(x,D)→sueandwin(x)`

In words: *If any person x is hurt by D, then x sues and will probably win.*

❑   Rule 2) `ThereExists x such that hurtby(x,D) & sueandwin(x)→ForAll y not mayuse(y,D)`

In words: *If at least one person x is hurt by D and sues successfully, then nobody is able to use device D.* Admittedly, this is extreme, but in the United States, at least, we have almost arrived at that point.

❑   Rule 3) `ForAll x sick(x,S) & not mayuse(x,D)→die(x)`

In words: *If x has sickness S and x doesn't have device D, then x will die.* So, we're assuming the device D is important.

Warm-Up

 Let's see the consequences of some starting assumptions. Suppose we assume that D is new and there is an axiom:

```
ForAll Y newdevice(Y)→ThereExists x hurtby(x, Y)
```

What are the consequences?

Solution to Warm-Up

Given the axiom, the invention of D will inevitably lead to lawsuits and no savings in lives based on the following rules.

```
ThereExists x hurtby(x,D)→sueandwin(x)
ThereExists x such that hurtby(x,D) & sueandwin(x)→
ForAll y not mayuse(y,D)
ForAll x sick(x,S) & not mayuse(x,D)→die(x)
```

But this state of affairs is clearly undesirable. If D hurts very few people and saves many more, then D is overall good for society, at least in some utilitarian sense. Is there any way to take this into account in the lawsuits?

That is, suppose the judge at a trial could inform juries of the global cost-benefit history of the device. If the device has helped many more people than have been hurt, then the jury might take this into account. This could reduce the probability of success in lawsuits.

So, we enhance our logic with new predicates:

> `"MoreThanFraction(f) x ..."` means that more than a fraction f, including x, of people have the property represented by the ellipses.

> This then allows us to define a new rule 1 based on a fraction of, say, .02 (2.0%) for some device that is risky but overall very helpful:

❑   Rule 1) `MoreThanFraction(0.02) x hurtby(x,D)→sueandwin(x)`

In words: *If more than 2% of the people treated by device D are hurt, then those people can sue and win. For someone to sue and win, then that person must have been hurt and more than 2% must have been hurt.*

Using this rule and assuming only one person in a thousand is hurt, you can see that there are no lawsuits.

This may be the right idea, but a few problems remain. First, even if the effective probability of being hurt is in fact one quarter the threshold (say 0.005 in this case), the early history of the device could exceed the threshold.

45

1. If each patient has a 0.005 probability of being hurt, how likely is it to get one failure within the first 50 patients?

Hint: You can solve this using probability theory or by writing a small program that simulates this probability.

But overall success might cause us to miss a real lemon. After all, failures aren't necessarily independent. In the hands of some hospitals, for example, device D might be far more dangerous than in others. Suppose only 10 people out of 2,000 have been hurt overall, but all 10 were hurt in the same hospital, which had treated only 100 patients. What should be done? This is where your advice as a mathematician comes in. But first, suppose that the threshold for successful lawsuits is reduced to 1% per hospital.

2. Suppose that 18 people out of 4,000 have been hurt by the device. There are eight hospitals, each of which has treated 500 patients. What is the likelihood that at least one hospital exceeds a 1% test, i.e., has 6 patients who were hurt, even if the underlying chance of failure were in fact independent of hospital and is 0.005 per patient?

3. Suppose the distribution of patients were much more skewed, with seven hospitals having treated only 200 patients each and the remaining one having treated all the rest. How likely is it that at least one of those smaller hospitals had hurt three people or more under the same conditions (i.e., 18 people who were hurt overall and the underlying chance of failure is 0.005 per patient)?

So far, these cases have made the lawsuits look frivolous. After all, even if the ground probability of being hurt is 0.005 and the hospitals are all equally careful, hospitals are quite likely to be vulnerable to lawsuits based on the threshold test. But suppose we fix this problem by increasing the threshold back to 2%. If the higher threshold test is met or exceeded in some hospital, then the likelihood that the 0.005 model is correct becomes so small that a statistically informed jury would infer that the hospital had not done its job.

4. Suppose we say that if a single hospital has more than 2% of bad outcomes, then that is a bad hospital. Assume that each hospital treats 500 patients. What is the likelihood for at least one hospital to hurt 10 or more people if the 0.005 hurt probability held and there were no bias in any hospital?

5. How would you answer the last question in the case that seven hospitals each treat only 200 patients and one treats 3,600?

The bottom line: If a hospital wants to offer the use of a new device, it should use it a lot.

The Box Chip Game

Sometimes a problem comes along for which a seemingly insignificant twist completely changes its character. In this puzzle, we design the odds for a new game similar to Reach for the Sky!

You have in front of you some even number n of chips each having a different color and you have also n identical, opaque latched boxes. As you watch, your adversary puts one chip in each box. He then puts all the boxes in a mixing bowl and tumbles them extensively. He then removes them and lays them out in front of you. The net effect is that you have no idea which box contains which color.

Here is what you bet on. For each color, you point to n/2 boxes where that color might be. You make all guesses about all colors before any box is opened. If you are correct about every color, you win. Otherwise you lose.

It might seem that your chances of winning are $(1/2)^n$, but you can do better.

Warm-Up

 Suppose there are two chips — blue and red — and two boxes. So you must identify the box for red and the box for blue. Which guesses can you make so your chances of being right in both guesses is 1/2?

Solution to Warm-Up

Guess red in, say, the left box and blue in the right box. You'll either be both correct or both wrong. You might as well be consistent about the two colors. It's no worse for you for both to be wrong than if one is wrong.

Let's see how that generalizes. Say there are four chips (n=4) whose colors are Black, White, Red, and Green. You are to guess two boxes for each chip. Number the boxes 1, 2, 3, and 4. Your guesses will be a simple list of box numbers for each color. For example,

> Black guess: 1, 2
>
> White guess: 2, 4
>
> Red guess: 1, 3
>
> Green guess: 3, 4

1. For four chips and two guesses per color, can you figure out a way to win at least 1/6 of the time, assuming all rearrangements are equally likely? (The example just given might not achieve this.)

2. What if there are six chips and three guesses per color?

3. How does this probability generalize for n chips (n even) and n/2 guesses per color?

Now here comes the twist. It's small, but it changes everything. Under the old rules, for each color you provide n/2 boxes as guesses. Under the new rules, for each color you provide an initial guess and a procedure for determining each next guess based on the actual color found by the previous guess.

Here is an example for Black in the case of four colors:

```
Start with box 1;
case result of first step is
    Black, then win
    Red, then try box 2
    White, then try box 3
    Green, then box 4
```

For convenience, we will abbreviate this as follows:

Black guess: 1; Black→win, Red→2, White→3, Green→4

You must provide all initial guesses and procedures before any checking occurs and the procedures may not share information. If every color is found in n/2 or fewer guesses, you win.

We might conceptualize the situation as follows: Each chip color is represented by an agent who follows a procedure like the one above, though different agents may follow different procedures. A given agent enters the room with the boxes, looks inside the boxes as dictated by his procedure, but doesn't otherwise disturb the boxes. He or she then leaves the room without being able to communicate with any other agent, unless he loses, in which case the game is over.

Continuing with this scenario: A judge determines whether that "procedural agent" has won or not. If all agents win, then you (the person betting) win. Otherwise, the house wins. It may seem surprising, but you can do a lot better under these new rules.

4. How well can you do in the case of four chips and two guesses under the procedural agent assumption? *(Hint: You can win over 40 percent of the time.)*

5. How well can you do if you have six chips and three guesses?

Feedback Dividends

Have you ever admired your own skill at navigating a narrow road at high speed? If not, imagine the following alternative method of travel: Study a detailed map of the same road, figure out how much the wheel should turn and the accelerator should be pressed at every time point, and then drive down the road blindfolded. Even without obstacles, this is beyond the memory and trigonometric capacity of most of us.

In fact, we're hardly conscious of the intellectual effort of driving. Perhaps the reason is that the act of driving consists of very short-term plans (few seconds at most) followed by adaptation based on eyesight. The driver has an overall goal — get to some destination — but the plan is incremental and adaptive. This requires less brainpower and is far more robust to changes in the environment.

Any person on the street understands this argument, but we require quantification. So to make this concrete, examine the following game. Consider a standard checkerboard having 8 rows and 8 columns as in Figure 1-9.

You want to go from row 1, column 4 (the black square above the S) to row 8, column 5 (the black square below the E). Each move goes from black square to black square and proceeds up a row and either to the left or right diagonally adjacent square. If you fall off the checkerboard or reach the top row without reaching the correct square, you lose.

At each move, you as player get to aim to go either right or left. You will achieve that step's aim with probability Pgood, whose values we will discuss in a minute. There are two kinds of strategies: FeedYes and FeedNo.

A FeedYes strategy can decide where to aim on the ith move after seeing the results of the first i-1 moves. A FeedNo strategy must decide where to aim at step i from the very beginning.

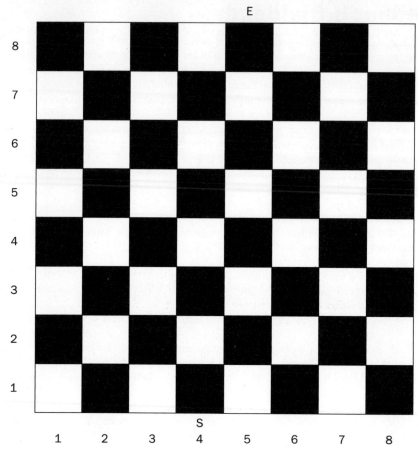

Figure 1-9: The goal is to go from the S to the E, always staying on black squares. Don't fall off the board.

Here is an example to show you the difference. Suppose you want to go from row 1, column 4 to row 3, column 4. Suppose that Pgood is 0.9. Then in the FeedYes strategy you might aim right the first move. If you in fact go right (probability 0.9), then you would aim left the second move. But if you go left on the first move (probability 0.1), you will aim right the second move. The net result is that you have a probability of 0.9 to hit your destination. In the FeedNo strategy, you might say something like "aim right the first move and aim left the second." There are two cases in which you would win with that strategy: You in fact move right in move 1 and left in move 2 (probability $0.9 \times 0.9 = 0.81$) or you move left in move 1 and right in move 2 (probability $0.1 \times 0.1 = 0.01$). So FeedNo has a probability of 0.82 of hitting the destination. Call the *feedback dividend* the probability of hitting the destination with the optimal FeedYes strategy divided by the probability of hitting it with the optimal FeedNo strategy. (Optimal means that you do as well as you can based on the probabilities.) In the example here, the feedback dividend is 0.9/0.81.

Warm-Up

 Are there any values of Pgood for which the feedback dividend is 1 regardless of source and destination?

Solution to Warm-Up

If Pgood were 0.5 or 1, the feedback dividend would be only one. In the first case, it doesn't matter where you aim. In the second, you don't need feedback. For all other Pgood values, the dividend will exceed one.

Now here is the full problem. You start at row 1, column 4 and you want to hit row 8, column 5.

1. If Pgood is 0.9, what is the probability of hitting row 8, column 5 using the FeedYes strategy and using the FeedNo strategy?

2. For which value of Pgood does the feedback dividend reach its greatest value? What is the feedback dividend in that case?

You may be surprised by the result of this second question. It's not intuitive at all.

3. If we cut off the three rightmost columns and the two leftmost columns, then which value of Pgood would give the highest feedback dividend? Assume that falling off the board gives a certain loss.

INFERENCE

What are you thinking?

Number Clues

Mind Games

Refuse and Reveal

A Biting Maze

Mad Mix

Number Clues

A certain number theorist has recently disappeared. His safe may contain papers that would lead police to his whereabouts. The trouble is that his safe will self-destruct if it is forced open. So we must infer the combination.

He has left a few hints. They involve pairs of numbers. Each pair, p and q, has a product (p × q), a greatest common divisor [gcd(p,q)], and a least common multiple [lcm(p,q)].

Consider, for example, p = 10 and q = 25. The greatest common divisor gcd(p,q) = 5, because both 10 and 25 are divisible by 5, but not by any number greater than 5. ("Divisible by" always implies a zero remainder.) The least common multiple lcm(p,q) = 50, because 50 is divisible by 10 and by 25, but no positive number less than 50 is divisible by both 10 and 25. So the greatest common divisor has all prime factors in common to p and q, in this case 5 alone. The least common multiple has the prime factors contained by either, in this case 2, 5, and 5.

The number theorist has left hints obeying the following rules:

i. These hints concern pairs of positive whole numbers p and q. For every pair, $p \leq q$.

ii. Each of p and q has two digits (i.e., between 10 and 99 inclusive).

Warm-Up

Suppose I tell you that q = 18, p is unknown, but gcd(p,q) = 6 and lcm(p,q) = 36. What is p?

Solution to Warm-Up

The factors of 36 are 2, 2, 3, and 3. The factors of 18 are 2, 3, and 3. The factors of 6 are 2, 3. So, we know that p has at least 2 and 3, because gcd(p,q) = 6 so 6 must divide p. Further, since lcm(p,q) = 36, either p or q has to have two 2s. Because q doesn't, p must, so p has factors 2, 2, and 3. Therefore p = 12.

Here are the first three hints, given stipulations (i) and (ii) above.

1. For the first p, q pair, lcm(p,q) = 60, p × q = 240. What are p and q?

2. The product of p and q is 140. gcd(p,q) = 2. What are p and q?

3. There is a pair p and q whose lcm(p,q) = 35. What are p and q?

The number theorist left another hint that the police have just decrypted: "If you've gotten this far, then you are doing well. Here now is one last hint."

4. The sequence of numbers that opens the safe is a sequence of five numbers from the hints. The sequence enjoys the following property: The greatest common divisors between neighbors of the sequence strictly increase as one proceeds from left to right in the sequence, but all greatest common divisors are single digits. What is the sequence that opens the safe?

Mind Games

You and I play a game that bears a strong family resemblance to the board game *Mastermind*. I think of a five binary digit secret number, e.g., 10101. You are allowed to pose questions about bit sequences of length five. Such a question is called a "bit question." My responses will report how many bits in your guess have their correct value in the correct place.

For example, if your bit question is 10110 and my secret is 10101, then three of your bits (the first three, though I won't tell you that) are in the correct place with their correct value. On the other hand, I could have other secret numbers that are consistent with the three-are-correct answer such as 00100.

Warm-Up

In fact, how many would be consistent with the answer of three correct for a bit question of 10110?

Solution to Warm-Up

Ten answers would be consistent. They would be: 10101, 10011, 10000, 11111, 11100, 11010, 00111, 00100, 00010, and 01110.

Warm-Up 2

If you guessed 10110 and were told that all five were incorrect, then which possibilities would there be?

Solution to Warm-Up 2

Only one sequence is consistent with that answer: 01001. Just reverse all the bits.

Warm-Up 3

If I give you the following answers, what is the secret number?

00000 — 2 correct

01000 — 1 correct, so second bit must be 0

00100 — 3 correct, so you know x01xx

01110 — 3 correct, so x011x

11100 — 1 correct, so 0011x

00001 — 3 correct, so last bit is 1 (compare with first response)

Solution to Warm-Up 3

Therefore, the secret number is 00111. These questions don't follow any particular systematic procedure, however. We should be able to do better.

---

1. What is the smallest number of bit questions sufficient to determine a five-bit sequence, no matter what it is? Remember that none of your bit questions need be correct. You just need to know how to crack the secret at the end.

   Hint: A five question solution is not too hard to find, so try that first. You can do better, however.

2. Suppose we change the game to make it a little more difficult: You ask some number of questions and then I answer them all after you have asked all your questions. In that case, how many bit questions are sufficient?

I've become decidedly less friendly. You pose an initial bit question, to which I give no response at all—ever. As with question 2, I answer all your questions after you have asked the last one. After that, I give you only "low info" answers, consisting of one of three responses:

(i) You have the same number correct as in the last bit question (S).

(ii) You have more correct than in the last bit question (+).

(iii) You have fewer correct than in the last bit question (-).

That's all I say. The term "correct" here still means correct bit in the correct position.

3. Given that the low info answers come at the end and there is no answer at all to the first bit question, is it possible to find the secret number, no matter what it is? If so, how many bit questions (counting the first one) do you need to pose in order to guarantee finding the secret number?

4. How many bit questions do you need, if you hear the low info answers immediately after posing them?

5. How does this generalize if the code is N digits long, but the digits could be base b for some b > 2? For example, b could be 10 and all digits 0 through 9 would be allowed. I have a solution when all answers come at the end, but that requires 1 + (b-1) × N questions. I don't think it's optimal.

Refuse and Reveal

One of the approaches to understanding a large amount of data is to characterize it using a few numbers. Statistics such as minimum, maximum, and the various kinds of averages tell you global properties. Sometimes they are enough to reveal information about individuals. This is why databases that give only statistical information are an issue for privacy advocates: Enough statistical questions can reveal personal data.

Consider a simple game between a questioner Quentin and a responder Rosalba. Quentin can ask only about global properties of a group of numbers, e.g., are they all whole numbers, are they distinct, and the statistics — mean, median, minimum, and maximum.

Rosalba always tells the truth. She may refuse to answer, however, if she knows the answer may divulge all the numbers. As we'll see, the refusal to answer may itself divulge all the numbers. Sometimes, she will volunteer information just for the fun of it.

Warm Up

> Rosalba: "I have five integers, all distinct."
>
> Quentin: "What is the minimum?"
>
> Rosalba: "15."
>
> Quentin: "What is the maximum?"
>
> Rosalba: "I won't tell, because you would know everything."

 What are the numbers?

Solution to Warm-Up

Because the numbers are all distinct, the maximum would tell everything only if it were 19. Then the collection consists of 15, 16, 17, 18, and 19. Okay, this was easy, but the deductions will get more interesting.

Before we go on, though, let me remind you of the definition of the mean and median. The *mean* of a collection of numbers is their sum divided by the number in the collection. For example the mean of 20, 22, 22, 40, and 101 is $205/5 = 41$. The *median* is the middle number in the sorted order, so 22 for this example. That is, the median is the middle in a sorted ordering of the values (our examples will always have an odd number of values).

1. Rosalba: "I have five integers that may or may not be distinct."

Quentin: "What is the minimum?"

Rosalba: "20."

Quentin: "Which of these would not allow me to infer all their values: number distinct, mean, maximum, or median?"

Rosalba: "Only the median."

Quentin: "Great. I know the numbers."

59

What are they?

2. Rosalba: "I have seven integers that may or may not be distinct."

Quentin: "What is the minimum?"

Rosalba: "20."

Quentin: "Which of these are you willing to tell me (i.e., would not allow me to infer all their values): mean, median, and maximum?"

Rosalba: "All of them."

Quentin: "Ok, what is the maximum?"

Rosalba: "21."

Quentin: "I know which of mean and median you're willing to tell me now."

Which? Why?

3. Rosalba: "Can you find some situation in which I would be happier to tell you the mean rather than the median?"

Quentin: "Could you give me a hint?"

Rosalba: "In an example I can think of, there are three numbers, two of them distinct." Give it a try.

4. Rosalba: "Can you find some situation in which all of minimum, maximum, mean, and median are necessary and sufficient to find the identities of five numbers that are all integers?"

Rosalba: "So far we've been playing games with just a few numbers. I've given you hints and you've been able to infer them all. But just a handful of numbers are not interesting. Let's try for more.

"Before we do that, let me define one new global property: the *total distance* to a point. Let's say we have the five numbers 10, 15, 20, 30, 60. The total distance to a point — say, 22 — is the sum of (22-10), (22-15), (22-20), (30-22), and (60-22). Mathematically, the total distance to x from a set of numbers is the sum of the absolute values of the differences between each number and x.

5. Rosalba: "Now we are ready. There are 17 numbers that are not all distinct. Their minimum is 30, mean is 34, and median is 35."

Quentin: "What is their total distance to 35?"

Rosalba: "I won't tell you, but the total distance to 35 is five less than the total distance to 38. Whoops! I shouldn't have told you that."

Quentin laughing: "You're right. Now I know the numbers."

What are they?

6. How would your answer to this question change if there were 1701 numbers, but otherwise the same information as in the previous question?

A Biting Maze

A conventional maze is a set of walls or hedges enclosing roughly a rectangular plot of ground. One enters from the outside of the rectangle and wants to exit somewhere else to the outside of the rectangle. A well-known strategy to guarantee to exit such a maze is to keep your left hand on the wall and walk forward. Eventually you will reach the exit.

For example, consider the simple maze in Figure 1-10.

Exit

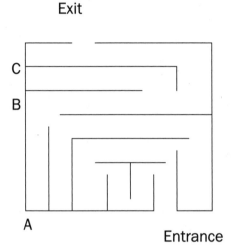

A

Entrance

Figure 1-10: You are to travel this maze from entrance to exit by keeping your left hand on the wall and walking forward. Will you make it?

Keep your left hand on the wall at the entrance at the bottom and walk forward. This will lead you under the T shaped wall (though you will never touch it), up and above the entrance to the right, eventually to the bottom left corner (labeled A), then B, and then the dead end at C. But the left hand strategy will lead you out of this dead end until you will finally approach the exit from the left. This is certainly not the most efficient way to go through the maze, but it is guaranteed to work.

Warm-Up

Can you see why this strategy will always work on any maze whose entrance and exit are gaps in the outside wall?

Solution to Warm-Up

Imagine that the exterior wall surfaces of the maze are painted black and the interior wall surfaces are painted white. Imagine that as you walk, you draw a line with your left hand using a crayon. Even though your path may not seem to be efficient, it ensures that you never go over the same section of white wall twice until you get to the exterior of the maze

61

(and hit a black surface). There is clearly only a finite amount of white wall surface between the entrance and the first exterior point of the maze. Therefore, you will eventually get out. (By symmetry, a right hand on the right wall will also work.)

This next puzzle, however, escapes the limitations of the physical world because the maze is on the Web. So there is no analogue to putting your left hand on the wall—even if you always go left, you could go in a circle.

The first Web page is at `http://cs.nyu.edu/cs/faculty/shasha/papers/mazebook .d/f43.html`. You want to get to a Web page that tells you (albeit in code) that you have arrived. There are hints along the way.

1.   The challenge is to find a route to the final page, and to decrypt the words and phrases on the way. There are hints in the encrypted words (they form a sentence about natural history) and in other parts of the Web page. Give it a try.

Mad Mix

Imagine we have two large reservoirs of fluids. One contains the liquid 'supertox' and one contains purified water. We want to get certain proportional mixtures of the two.

There is also a drain for waste. Supertox is very dangerous, however, so we'd like to pour as little down the drain as possible, even in dilute form. Supertox is polar, so supertox and water mix perfectly and instantly whenever one is poured into the other.

In addition, we have two opaque measuring vessels, one of 10 liters and one of 7. We call these the 10-vessel and the 7-vessel for short. There are no measurement lines on the vessels. When we fill a vessel from a reservoir, we fill it from a faucet, as our client is nervous about contamination from handling.

So we can fill a vessel to completion from a reservoir or we can pour liquid from one vessel to the other, stopping either when the receiving vessel is full or the source vessel is empty. We are allowed to pour pure water back in the water reservoir and to pour pure supertox back into the supertox reservoir.

Warm-Up

We want to create a 10-liter solution having 40% of supertox without pouring anything down the drain. How do we do it?

Solution to Warm-Up

Fill the 7-vessel with supertox. Pour into the 10-vessel. Fill the 7-vessel with supertox again. Pour into the 10-vessel until the 10-vessel is full. So we have 4 left in the 7-vessel. Pour the contents of the 10-vessel back into the supertox container. Pour the contents of the 7-vessel into the 10-vessel, and then fill the rest of the 10-vessel with water.

---

1. We want a mixture having 2.7 liters of supertox in a 3-liter mixture. We don't want to pour more than 10 liters of any liquid laced with supertox down the drain. How can we achieve this?

2. Can we get a mixture that is 2/9 supertox and the rest water without pouring any supertox down the drain?

Now, chemists require extremely precise mixtures, so let me explain our terminology with an example. A 25% concentration of supertox in the 10-liter container would correspond to 2.5 liters of supertox and 7.5 liters of water.

Also, we have a big empty bucket at our disposal that can hold over 100 liters, though we don't know exactly how big it is.

3. Can we get a 26% concentration of supertox in the 7-liter container?

4. Suppose that we want to get mixtures which are all supertox, 1/2 supertox, 1/3 supertox, 1/4 supertox, ... 1/50 supertox. You are allowed to specify the size of the two vessels. You may even include fractional sizes as long as the smallest vessel contains at least one liter and the largest contains at most 30 liters. In addition, you have the big bucket again with capacity over 100 liters. Which two vessel sizes would you choose in order to obtain each of these mixtures? Given those vessel sizes and given a target mixture, how would you obtain it?

OPTIMIZATION

Doing more with less

Dig That!

Preferential Romance

No Change for the Holidays

Quiet in the Depths

Dig That!

Imagine a road grid with seven rows as in Figure 1-11.

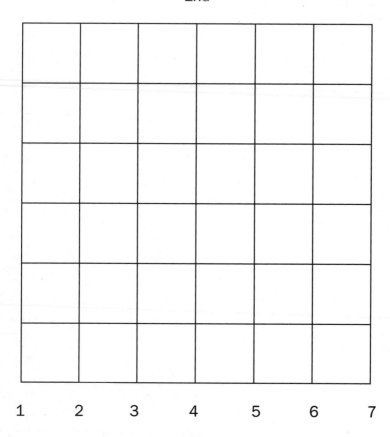

End

| 1 | 2 | 3 | 4 | 5 | 6 | 7 |

Start

Figure 1-11: Somewhere between Start and End in this road network is an eight-block tunnel some bad guys have built.

Some bad guys have placed a tunnel from the bottom, beginning at the intersection marked Start in the south, and ending at End in the north. The tunnel follows the path of the roads somehow but may wind around. It is also a simple path (no dead ends and no loops along the way). You want to probe a minimum number of times and yet be able to find the exact route of the tunnel.

A probe device takes an hour to set up. We can set them up at intersections or in the middle of the street. If you establish a probe on a street, you can tell whether the tunnel follows the street. If you set the probe up at an intersection, you can tell whether the tunnel passes through the intersection, and, if so, according to the engineering team, which adjacent streets it goes to.

1. If the tunnel is at most eight blocks long and begins at Start and ends at End, then what is the minimum number of probe devices you would need to guarantee to determine the precise route of the tunnel in one hour?

2. If you had only one probe, what is the minimum time it would take to guarantee to determine the outcome, assuming you could move the probe every hour?

Suppose all a probe could tell was whether a tunnel ran under it or not, but could not tell the direction. In the engineering jargon, suppose we had point probes rather than directional probes.

3. If the tunnel is at most eight blocks long and begins at Start and ends at End, then what is the minimum number of point probe devices you would need to place to guarantee to determine the precise route of the tunnel in one hour?

Hint: Remember that you can place probes at intersections or in the middle of streets.

Suppose you have two hours, but you are not allowed to reuse any probe?

4. How few point probes could you use over two hours to guarantee to find the tunnel?

Preferential Romance

A certain marriage counseling service called Marriage Success, or MS for short, advises couples on how to get along better. MS's idea is simple: Each spouse writes down his/her preferences about various criteria of common interest. "Our criteria go beyond those elements of physical appearance and passion that guide early romance and tend to blind judgment. We want to understand your values as you live day to day. The happy couple is the one whose preferences are compatible or can be made compatible."

Here are some of the positive qualities each person might wish a spouse to have: biker (B), cultured (C), enthusiastic (E), foodie (F), hiker (H), juggler (J), kayaker (K), movies (M), organized (O), puzzles (P), rich (R), theatre (T), and windsurfer (W).

Suppose X and Y are qualities of people. X→Y implies a preference for X to Y. Preferences are transitive, so X →Y and Y→Z implies X→Z. Two people are *fully compatible* if their preferences are consistent. The test for consistency is that there is some list of qualities that reflects both of their preferences. If two people aren't fully compatible, then perhaps at least they are *passably compatible*, which means they would be fully compatible if each spouse dropped at most one preference.

Warm-Up

Suppose Bob's preferences are

> K→M→P, and R→T

and Alice's preferences are

> O→P→R and W→T.

 Then would they be fully compatible?

Solution to Warm-Up

Yes. Ignoring the qualities not mentioned (because they can be put anywhere), here is a consistent ordering for these preferences: KOMPRWT. This is consistent in the sense that for every preference X→Y, X comes before Y in the list. On the other hand, if Alice added the preference R→M, then the couple would not be compatible because P→R and R→M implies P→M, but Bob has M→P. If Bob drops his M→P preference, then we would be left with:

> Bob: K→P, and R→T
>
> Alice: O→P→R→M and W→T.

This could yield the following consistent ordering, among others: KOPRMWT. So Bob and Alice would then be passably compatible.

MS requires that each person be consistent in that he or she has no cyclic preferences of the form X is better than Y which is better than Z which is better than X. The bad news is that the real Bob and Alice are both very opinionated, so they have each listed many preferences, so many, in fact, that I have drawn Figures 1-12 and 1-13 to illustrate.

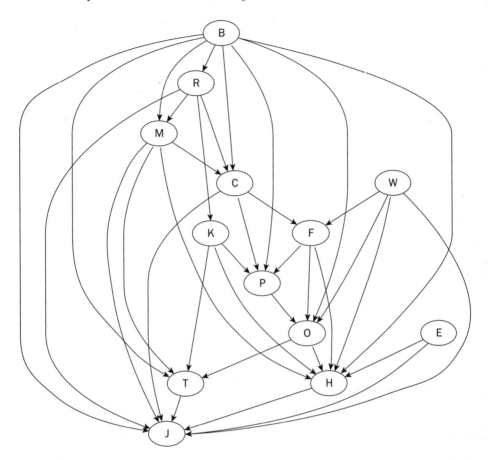

Figure 1-12: Bob's preferences in life. Note that he has no preferences for certain qualities, e.g., he has not said whether he prefers Alice to be cultured or to be a windsurfer.

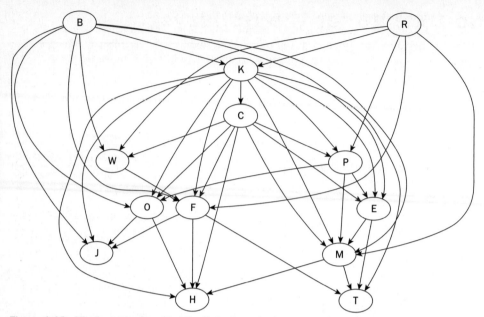

Figure 1-13: Alice's preferences in life. Note that she has no preference about whether Bob is rich or a biker.

1. Are Bob and Alice compatible, passably compatible, or neither? After dropping the smallest number of edges in zero, one, or both spouse's preferences, try to find a consistent ordering.

2. *[For the entrepreneurial at heart]* Can you describe an algorithm for the counseling company to use to help marriages in distress? That is, try to find a method so spouses have to drop as few preferences as possible.

No Change for the Holidays

Have you ever noticed that if a teenager is given $50 to buy a $20 item, no money comes back? Some other item was just *so* essential...

In this puzzle, we provide the teenager with a good excuse. *Artiste* and street vendor Claude sells beautiful handmade items for $100 or less but refuses to give change.

You have no cash, but you have three checks. You will make them out to Claude in whole dollar amounts. Your teenager is to give Claude the combination of checks that is the minimum amount more than necessary for the purchase price. For example, if you give your child a $50 check, a $30 check, and a $20 check and the item costs $53, your child will give Claude the $50 and $20 checks and Claude will keep the $17 in change in addition to the purchase price.

You like Claude's stuff, but you very much begrudge him his "I keep the change" attitude. So you'd like to minimize the amount he keeps beyond the purchase price.

Warm-Up

 If you knew that the item in question cost either $20, $40, $50, or $60, which combination of three check amounts could you give in order to leave no change for Claude?

Solution to Warm-Up

$20, $40, and $50 is one among many solutions. Claude will not be able to keep anything in change.

---

1. If you did not know how much the purchase price is except that it is a whole number amount between $1 and $100 inclusive, which amounts would you write on your three checks in order to minimize Claude's change?

2. Suppose Claude publishes his four whole-number prices in an advertisement that you see. Can you show how he can guarantee to do so in such a way that at least one item will yield him non-zero change no matter which check amounts you write?

Quiet in the Depths

The need for near-silence in a submarine leads to strict procedures. As a submarine captain explained, "One of our drills, in case we are under conditions of extreme radio silence inside the submarine, is to exchange information among our five key departments. Naturally, we can't tell you which those are.

"Each department consists of five sailors. Our basic protocol works as follows: As captain, I request certain information by broadcasting the request to all departments; each department responds with a number that is sent only to the captain (no broadcast); then the captain may broadcast a number; and so on. Remember, the captain broadcasts; the others don't.

"To demonstrate, the departments will exchange very few messages with me — as few as possible — in order for me to determine some information. Naturally, we can't reveal to you the nature of such information, but my first officer has come up with a sanitized version."

Warm-Up

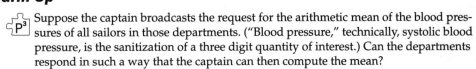 Suppose the captain broadcasts the request for the arithmetic mean of the blood pressures of all sailors in those departments. ("Blood pressure," technically, systolic blood pressure, is the sanitization of a three digit quantity of interest.) Can the departments respond in such a way that the captain can then compute the mean?

Solution to Warm-Up

Each department calculates the mean of its sailors' blood pressures and reports that number. The captain computes the sum of these means and divides by five. This works because each department has the same number of sailors (otherwise the captain would have had to weight each reported mean by the number of sailors in that department).

Okay, that was pretty easy. It turns out they weren't so interested in the mean as in the median. (The mean is too sensitive to outliers.) But the median itself wasn't necessary, simply a "blood pressure" among the 10 middle values of the 25.

1. Assuming blood pressures are three digits long, can each department report one three digit number so that the captain can infer a blood pressure among the 10 middle blood pressures of the 25 sailors?

2. The captain wants to find some blood pressure value that is sure to be less than or equal to the median and some blood pressure value that is sure to be greater than or equal to the median. Using the assumptions of the first question, can the captain infer such a value after one three-digit report from each department?

Solutions

Solution to Sweet Tooth

1. How does Jeremy maximize the amount of cake he gets, given these rules? How much will he get?

Jeremy cuts the first cake in the fractions f and 1-f, where f is at least 1/2. Then if Marie chooses first, Jeremy will get 1 1/4 cakes from the last two by the argument of the warm-up. If Marie chooses second, Jeremy will get f and then will divide the last two cakes in half. So, f + 1/2 + 1/2 = (1 - f) + 1 1/4. That is, f + 1 = 2 1/4 - f. 2f = 1 1/4. That is f = 5/8. Therefore, Jeremy will receive 1 5/8 cakes and Marie will receive 1 3/8 cakes.

2. Suppose there were seven cakes and Marie got the first choice for six of the seven cakes. Who has the advantage? By how much?

There is an inductive pattern. If for k cakes where Marie gets the first choice in all but one, Jeremy still has an advantage A (that is, Jeremy would receive A more cake than Marie among those k), then Jeremy will still have an advantage for k+1 cakes. Here is why: Jeremy, knowing that he will have an advantage of A if Marie chooses first for the first cake, cuts the first piece into two pieces 1/2 + A/4 and 1/2 - A/4. If Marie chooses the piece having 1/2 + A/4, then Jeremy will suffer a disadvantage of A/2 for that first cake, but will gain an advantage of A for the remaining k cakes, so have a net advantage of A/2. By contrast, if Marie chooses to go second for the first cake, then Jeremy will cut the remaining cakes in half. Again he will have an overall advantage of A/2. Thus, Jeremy's advantages from 1/2 for two cakes, to 1/4 for three cakes, to 1/8 for four cakes, to ... 1/64 for seven cakes.

3. Is there any way to ensure that each child receives the same amount of cake, assuming Jeremy always cuts?

Yes, simply make it so Marie gets the first choice every time. That will force Jeremy to cut evenly every time.

Solution to Byzantine Bettors

1. Now suppose there are only three advisors and only one of them always tells the truth. Again, you can make three even money bets. You start with $100. How much can you guarantee to win?

If the vote is two against one, then bet x on the majority. If you lose, the advisor in the minority must be the truth-teller so you can bet everything on the next two bets by following the advice of the truth-teller. This gives you $4 \times (100 - x)$. If you win by following the majority the first time, you should disregard the advisor in the minority and you'll have 100+x after the first bet. In the next bet, if the remaining two agree, you bet everything because one must always tell the truth. But if not, you'll find out who is telling the truth by betting nothing. On the last bet, you follow the truth teller and end up with at least $2 \times (100 + x)$.

Setting $4 \times (100 - x) = 2 \times (100 + x)$, you conclude that $6x = 200$ or $x = 33\ 1/3$. Plugging that into either equation corresponds to handling both cases when the vote is two against one. Thus, in either case, you end up with 2 2/3 of what you start with — a total of $266.66.

2. **What can you guarantee to win in four bets, with four advisors, three of whom can lie at will, and one of whom must tell the truth at least three out of four times?**

In this case, unfortunately, you cannot guarantee anything. The reason is that your "advisors" can arrange it so that you never have a reason to choose one outcome over the other. Call the advisors A, B, C, and D.

> **Bet 1:** AB advise 0; CD advise 1.
>
> **Outcome:** 1, so A and B have each lied once.
>
> **Bet 2:** AC advise 0; BD advise 1.
>
> **Outcome:** 1, so A has lied twice so is a definite liar.
>
> B and C have each lied once.
>
> D has not yet lied.
>
> **Bet 3:** BD advise 0; AC advise 1.
>
> **Outcome:** 1, so B is a definite liar. C and D have each lied once.
>
> **Bet 4:** AC advise 0 and BD advise 1.

Notice that, in bet 2, if you had bet on 1 but the outcome had been 0 (because the advisors had changed the written result), then B would be out, A and C would have lied once, and C would have never lied. This is symmetrical to what happened with just a rearrangement of labels. So, you would have learned no more if the outcome had been 0. Similarly, in the third bet, if the outcome were 0, then D and B would both be possible partial truth tellers in bet 4. Thus, no series of outcomes ever teaches you whom to trust. The advisors can arrange it so that every bet you make is a loser.

3. **Under the reliability conditions of one partial truth teller who tells the truth four out of five times and three liars at will, but assuming you have five bets, can you guarantee to end with at least $150?**

Even with five bets, the advisors can keep you from winning much. Their strategy starts similarly to their strategy when you had only four bets.

> **Bet 1:** AB advise 0; CD advise 1.
>
> **Outcome:** 1, so A and B have each lied once.
>
> **Bet 2:** AC advise 0; BD advise 1.
>
> **Outcome:** 1, so A has lied twice so is a definite liar.
>
> B and C have each lied once.
>
> D has not yet lied.
>
> **Bet 3:** BC advise 0; AD advise 1.

75

Now, we must do a case analysis.

Case 1: Suppose you bet nothing on bet 3. Suppose the outcome is 1. Now you know that D is the partial truth teller because everyone else has lied twice. However, D may still lie once. If D advises 1 in bet 4 and you bet x on 1, then if $x < 50$ and D tells the truth in bet 4, you cannot bet anything on bet 5 because D could lie then. If $x \geq 50$, then D could lie in bet 4 and you will never do better than regain your original capital. So, if you bet nothing, you cannot attain $150.

Case 2: Suppose you bet something on 0 in bet 3. Then your situation is as in case 1, only worse.

Case 3: Suppose you bet $x on 1 in bet 3. If $x < \$12.50$, then suppose further the outcome is in fact 1 and you bet $y in bet 4 on the outcome offered by D and $x + y < 50$. Then, if you win in bet 4, you cannot bet in bet 5 (because D may lie). If $x + y > 50$, then $y > \$37.50$, so if you lose bet 4, you will have less than $75, so cannot attain $150 in bet 5. Therefore $x \geq \$12.50$.

Now suppose that you bet $x on 1 in bet 3, but the outcome is 0. Then you have $100 - x$ and you know that B, C, and D have all lied once. In bet 4, two of them must advise one outcome and one must advise the other. Let's say you bet $z on the outcome suggested by the majority. Then $x + z \leq 25$; otherwise losing in bets 3 and 4 will leave you less than $75, making it impossible to attain $150 in bet 5. But this implies $z \leq \$12.50$ and therefore if you win in bet 4, you will have at most $100 and D can still lie in bet 5. If you bet with the minority in bet 4, the majority could be telling the truth and then there would remain two advisors who have lied only once.

Therefore, you cannot guarantee to attain $150. In fact, a refinement of this argument shows you cannot even attain $134. Ivan Rezanka has argued that $133.33 can be guaranteed, but a short elegant proof is still missing.

Solution to A Touch of Luck

1. **Bob, Carol, and Alice play. Alice has 51 units, whereas Bob and Carol have 50 each. Bob must state his bet first, then Carol, and then Alice. Bob and Carol collude to share the reward if either wins. How can Bob and Carol maximize the probability that at least one of them wins if there is just one coin flip left?**

Bob bets 50 on heads and Carol bets 50 on tails. If Alice bets 49 or less, then she can't possibly win because even if she guesses the correct coin orientation, her 100 will equal the 100 of one of Bob or Carol. If Alice bets 50 or more on heads, then she wins on heads and Carol wins on tails. So, Bob and Carol can guarantee to have a 1/2 chance to win.

2. **Does the result change if Alice must state her bet first?**

If Alice bets 48 or less, then Bob and Carol bet as above. One of them will surely win. But if Alice bets at least 50, Bob and Carol can do no better than before. So, the result stays the same.

3. Suppose Bob has 51 units and Alice 50. There are two coin flips left. Bob bets first for the penultimate flip. Alice bets first for the last flip. Does Bob have more than a 1/2 chance of winning? If so, how much more?

Bob will win with probability 3/4. In the penultimate round, he bets nothing. No matter what Alice bets, she cannot exceed 100 units. If Alice loses in the penultimate round, then since she must state her bet first in the last round, Bob just bets as she does in that round and is guaranteed to win. If Alice wins in the penultimate round, then, in the last round, Bob simply bets all his units on the coin face opposite to the one Alice chooses. (If Alice doesn't bet in the last round, Bob can bet everything on, say, heads.) So Bob will win 3/4 of the time.

4. Suppose Bob has 51 units and Alice 50. Again, there are two coin flips left. This time, Alice bets first for the penultimate flip. Bob bets first for the last flip. Does Bob have more than a 1/2 chance of winning? If so, how much more?

Suppose Alice bets 2 on heads in the penultimate round. If Bob bets nothing or bets on tails and the penultimate flip lands on heads, then Alice wins for sure by using the strategy from the warm-up. If Bob bets all 51 on heads and the result is tails, then again Alice is sure to win on the last flip. If Bob bets anything on heads and the result is heads, then Bob has at most 102 and Alice has 52. In that case, on the last flip, Alice bets everything on the opposite face to Bob's and she will win 1/2 the time regardless of what Bob bets. So, Alice wins at least 1/2 the time and will win more often if Bob plays foolishly. A good move for Bob would be simply to bet the same amount as Alice on the same face (so 2 on heads if Alice bets 2 on heads) in the penultimate flip. He can then bet nothing on the last flip and be sure to win with probability 1/2.

5. Suppose Bob has 51 units and Alice 50. Again, there are two coin flips left. Again, Alice states her bet first in the penultimate round and Bob states his bet first in the final one. This time, Bob announces that he will bet 20 in the penultimate round, though he will wait to see Alice's bet before saying whether he will bet on heads or tails. Can Alice arrange to have more than a 1/2 chance to win?

Yes. Alice bets nothing in the penultimate round. If Bob loses, Alice wins for sure in the final round using the strategy of the second warm-up. If Bob wins, Alice bets everything on the coin face opposite to the one Bob chooses in the final round. She will win with probability 3/4.

6. Bob, Alice, Rino, and Juliana have 100 units each and there are two flips left. Each person is out to win — no coalitions. Bob and Alice have bet 100 on heads. Rino has bet 100 on tails. Juliana must now state her bet, knowing that she will state her bet first on the last flip. What are her chances of winning if she bets 90 on either heads or tails? What should she bet?

If Juliana bets 90, she has no hope of winning. If she bets 90 on heads and the outcome is heads, then Bob and Alice will each have 200 compared to her 180 after the first flip. If she then bets x on, say, heads, on the last flip, she knows that (i) Bob and Alice must split their bets on that last flip (because ties do them no good) and (ii) one of them can arrange to bet x or more on heads as well. Covered in this way, she has no chance of winning. If Juliana bets 90 on tails in the first flip and the outcome is tails, then Rino will cover her on the last flip.

So, Juliana should bet 100 on tails in the penultimate flip. If the outcome is tails, then she and Rino will each have a 1/2 chance to win in the last flip. Rino won't bet as she does, again because ties do him no good. So, overall Juliana can arrange to have a 1/4 chance of winning, but she must bet high.

John Trono and Tom Rokicki lent their always-helpful insight to these solutions.

> *Note: All questions relating to this Touch of Luck puzzle mentioned so far have paper-and-pencil solutions. But the general situation having multiple players, multiple rounds, and different initial wealths is still elusive. The person who can solve it would have to mix, I think, expertise in game theory with algorithmic insight.*

Solution to Information Gain

1. **Is it possible for Jordan to design a protocol to ensure that each of his friends will raise the correct number of fingers? If so, explain it. If not, does Jordan have a high probability of winning?**

Jordan's team can win for sure. This time, by prior agreement, all the mathematicians will know: Ariana represents 0 if she receives a blue ticket and 5 if she receives red; Bob represents 1 for blue and 6 for red; Caroline represents 2 for blue and 7 for red; David represents 3 for blue and 8 for red; and Ellen represents 4 for blue and 9 for red.

Jordan adds up all the numbers on all the hats. He divides them by 10 and takes the remainder. For example, suppose the numbers are 3, 2, 7, 9, and 5. He adds them up and gets 26. The remainder after dividing by 10 is 6.

He sends a ticket reflecting the remainder value to the appropriate person. In this example he would send a red ticket to Bob to represent 6.

Now each mathematician adds up the other numbers and then derives his or her own number as the unique value to make the remainder work out.

In this example, Caroline would have a 7 on her hat. She would see 3, 2, 9, and 5. Adding those up, she would get 19. She knows the final remainder has to be 6, so she would hold up 7 fingers.

Solution to Reach for the Sky!

1. **What would be a good strategy for the $100,000 Reach for the Sky! game, where you have three captures? Using that strategy, what would be your chance of winning?**

Following the idea of the sultan's daughters problem, we will express our protocols in terms of three numbers in increasing order: n_1, n_2, and n_3. The idea is to reject the paper values in the first n_1 balls, then choose the first ball whose paper value is greater than the highest of those in the first n_1 balls. Call the ball number of the first capture b_1 (so $b_1 > n_1$).

If b1 > n2, then make the second capture at a ball whose paper value is a greater number than any paper value seen in the first b1 balls. Otherwise (when b1 ≤ n2), reject all paper values until the first n2 balls (altogether) have been seen and then make the second capture occur at a ball whose paper value is greater than any seen so far in the first n2. Call the position of the second capture b2.

If b2 > n3, then choose, for the third capture, the paper value greater than any seen before position b2. Otherwise, reject until position n3 and then pick the next one better than any seen before the first n3. Call the position of the third capture b3.

Of course, if the highest value happens to be in the first n1 balls, then you will never choose anything, but it wouldn't help to do so anyway. That suggests that it is useful to make n1 rather small.

For 100 balls in total and 3 captures, you win roughly 68 percent of the time if you set n1, n2, and n3 to be 14, 32, and 64, respectively.

Consider, for example, the following sequence of 100 values where each dollar amount written by your adversary has been replaced by its rank. That is, the highest dollar figure is replaced by 99 and the lowest by 0.

```
78 3 80 90 25 95 51 27 57 40 65 48 55 72 26 73 54 31 15 2 89 61 97 98 8
50 38 18 88 52 4 42 68 16 62 9 94 99 20 28 56 58 76 93 10 96 63 35 81 91
66 11 30 5 0 24 82 29 41 12 47 71 44 92 43 32 85 84 7 59 60 86 69 21 83
79 64 67 74 37 1 46 22 19 33 39 87 45 36 13 23 75 34 70 53 49 77 17 6 14
```

The b1 position value in this case would be 23 where the value 97 is found, because 97 is the first value larger than 95, which is the largest of the first 14 numbers. The b2 value would be 38 where 99 is found and the third capture then is irrelevant.

The bottom line: Take the bet.

There may be an elegant analytical way to solve this problem as there is for the original sultan's daughters problem, but the puzzle is so amenable to programming, it didn't seem worth it. Simply choose ascending triples and then, for each triple, generate 10,000 random permutations of the numbers between 0 and 99 (the ranks) and see how often you win. Such a strategy is not limited to triples, obviously.

2. How would your answer change if there were 1,000 lottery balls?

For 1,000 balls with three captures, you win roughly 66 percent of the time if you set n1, n2, and n3 to be 141, 317, and 650 respectively. So, you should still take the bet. Isn't it amazing that the odds stay so good?

Solution to Pork Politics

1. Which coalitions might form?

A and C will form a coalition together. C prefers A to any other coalition, because C will get the most money in that case. A also prefers C.

2. How strong a majority should B prefer (51%, 67%, or 75%) in order for B to receive as much money as possible?

67% would be best for B. Then B would be part of the A, B, E coalition and B would get the fraction 25/70 of the money. A also would get more with this coalition than with any other winning coalition of which A would be a part. If the cutoff were 75%, A would team up with C, D, and E. B would get nothing.

Solution to Social Games

1. How would punishment have to change to eliminate cheats-cheats as a Nash equilibrium?

If punishment were to increase to -9, then the upper right corner would give Alice $(4 \times 0.9) + ((-9) \times 0.1)$. The bottom right corner would give an expected gain of 0. That yields the matrix:

	Alice Honest	Alice Cheats
Bob Honest	3, 3	0, 2.7
Bob Cheats	2.7, 0	0, 0

In this case, if Alice cheats, Bob receives the same gain whether he cheats or not. So, the lower right and the upper right are the same from Bob's point of view. If Bob decides not to cheat, then the game state will move to the upper right and from there to the upper left. To encourage this, you could make the punishment even slightly more negative than -9 (e.g., -9.01).

2. If you are a public policy maker and you want to limit the punishment for cheating to -5, how much must you increase the probability of catching criminals to maintain the upper left as the only Nash equilibrium?

Suppose punishment is reduced to -5 and the probability of punishment is raised to 17 percent. Then the expected gain for Alice from cheating is $(0.83 \times 1) + (0.17 \times -5) = -0.02$ in the bottom right state. In the upper right corner, the expected gain will be $(0.83 \times 4) + (0.17 \times -5) = 2.47$.

	Alice Honest	Alice Cheats
Bob Honest	3, 3	0, 2.47
Bob Cheats	2.47, 0	-0.02, -0.02

So the only Nash equilibrium is the upper left.

3. Assuming a 10 percent likelihood of being caught, is there a punishment value that would cause the only Nash equilibrium to be the upper right state (Alice commits crime but Bob does not)?

Under the assumption of a 10 percent likelihood of being caught, let's say the punishment is -9.01. Then the lower right has an effective value of $(-9.01 \times 0.1) + (1 \times 0.9) = -0.001$. The upper right has (for Alice) a value of $(-9.01 \times 0.1) + (4 \times 0.9) = 2.699$, which we'll approximate to 2.7.

This yields a game matrix of:

	Alice Honest	Alice Thief
Bob Honest	5, 2	0, 2.7
Bob Thief	2.7, 0	-0.001, -0.001

So, Alice will take the matrix to the upper right corner. Bob can rail about immorality, but Alice sees it all as a game.

4. Still assuming a 10 percent likelihood of being caught, what must the punishment be to force Alice to stay honest?

Recall the game matrix relevant to this question:

	Alice Honest	Alice Thief
Bob Honest	5, 2	0, 4
Bob Thief	4, 0	1, 1

If punishment increases to, say, -17 (which might represent cutting off the hand of a thief who steals bread), then the game matrix becomes:

	Alice Honest	Alice Thief
Bob Honest	5, 2	0, 1.9
Bob Thief	1.9, 0	-0.8, -0.8

The only Nash equilibrium is the upper left.

Solution to Escape Management

1. The police want to control T's direction at only five intersections. They know that T is extremely motivated to escape. How long (in terms of single block steps) at most will it take T to arrive at either the northern or southern border?

Figure 1-14 shows most of the northern half. The situation is symmetric for the south. The police are represented by dashed arrows and the thief by solid arrows. The earliest T can escape is after traveling 22 blocks (which we call steps). This is the best possible for P because each southerly step that P forces requires for compensation at most one east-or-west plus one northerly step by T. Here is the calculation. T needs nine steps even without obstruction. Add to that one by P to change directions to east-or-west plus four southerly steps forced by P, each of which requires two compensatory steps by T. So the best possible strategy for P is $9 + 1 + (4 \times 3) = 22$.

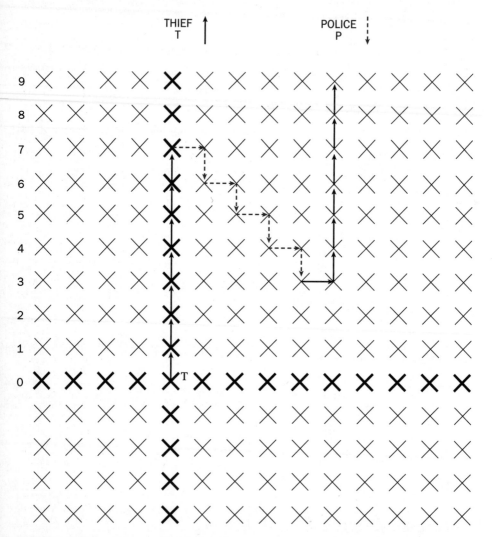

Figure 1-14: The northern half of the city T wants to escape from. The police are represented by dashed arrows and the thief by solid arrows. T leaves after 22 block steps.

2. Suppose that the police want to prevent T from reaching the northern or southern borders. Therefore the police plan to control T's direction m out of every n times for some m < n. What should m and n be to minimize the fraction of time P forces T to change directions while still preventing T from escaping?

The police can use a strategy more or less in the spirit of the solution to question 1. The idea is to let the thief go eight steps (to one step away from the northern border) and then to force the thief to go east (or west) and then south just as in the figure above. The thief then moves east or west and then the police force a move south again. The police eventually force the thief all the way down to row 1, but facing away from the northern border. This requires eight steps by the police and 15 steps by the thief. So the police intervene 8 times out of every 23.

3. **How does your answer change if T can escape by reaching any border, including the eastern and western ones?**

If the police intervene two times out of every four, then they can force the thief to stay in a six by six square around the center. Each time the thief goes, say, east and then north, the police force the thief to go west and then south. If the thief goes in a single direction, then the police force the thief to stay within the central six by six square. This plan clearly lacks subtlety, but it works. I see no better general solution, but maybe a clever reader will find one. If so, please let me know.

These solutions are due to Ivan Rezanka.

Solution to Flu Math

1. **As long as the government is in a compelling mode, what fraction should be required to take the vaccine in order to minimize the overall average risk?**

If a fraction f take the flu shot, then the death toll is $5f + 10(1-f)(1-f) = 5f + 10f^2 - 20f + 10$. That is, $10f^2 - 15f + 10$. This is minimized when $20f = 15$ or $f = 0.75$. At that point, we'd have a death toll of only $(5 \times 0.75) + (2.5 \times 0.25) = 4.375\%$. Notice, however, that those who don't take the vaccine have a probability of only 2.5% of dying whereas the ones who do take the flu shot have a 5% chance of dying.

2. **Under these conditions (no compulsion, full belief in government risk figures, selfishness), what percentage of people will take the flu shot?**

Exactly half (or maybe one less than half, given the bias towards inaction). Here is why. Take the ith person. If half have already taken the flu shot, then there is no reason to take it. Person i will die with a 5% probability if he or she takes the shot and will die with a 5% probability or less if he or she doesn't take the shot. If less than half have taken it and there are just enough people left for half to take it, then person i will take it for sure, because if he or she doesn't, the chances of living will be less than if he or she took the shot. We call this the "must-vaccinate" point.

3. **Suppose 25% of the population will not take the vaccine under any circumstances. Nobody else knows beforehand who they are. Then can you determine what percentage of people will in fact take the vaccine under the same assumptions?**

In this case, at most 50% will take the vaccine. Once 50% have taken the vaccine, nobody (neither a refuser nor a normal citizen) will take it. If fewer than 50% have taken the vaccine and we are at the must-vaccinate point, then a non-refuser will take the vaccine, but a refuser of course will not.

4. Again, the government will compel nobody. To which percentage should the risk of disease be inflated to achieve the vaccination level you determined in your answer to question 1?

The government wants f = 0.75 from the answer to 1. So if the initial perceived risk is R, each person will take the vaccine until R(1-f) = R 0.25 = 5%. So R = 20%. That is, if everyone believes the initial unvaccinated risk is 20%, then 75% of the people will take the vaccine.

Solution to Whipping Ice

1. Does Indy need more poles than the two shown by the dark circles in Figure 1-4 to go from the bottom to the top?

This solution requires two connections and disconnections to the same pole, as shown in Figure 1-15.

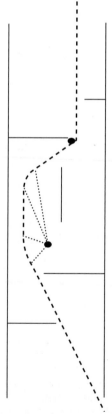

Figure 1-15: Indy uses the first pole both to straighten out and then eventually to curve in.

2. There are several L-shaped barriers and several objects (at the Xs) that Indy wants to collect in a game called Treasure Skater. What is the minimum number of poles he will need and where should he place them?

Four poles are enough. Figure 1-16 shows the basic solution. Notice that poles can be used many times.

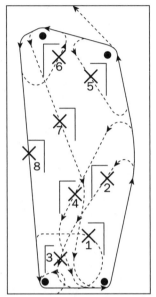

Figure 1-16: This is the route Indy should take starting from the bottom to win at Treasure Skater. The numbers indicate the order in which Indy visits the Xs. Notice that he does a sharp turn using the lower left pole and then uses that pole again to curve up to X1. He then uses the lower left pole and the lower right pole twice to swing to 2 and 3.

The tricky part is near the X labeled 4 (see Figure 1-17).

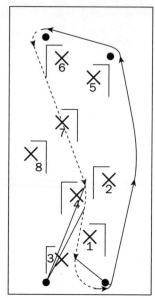

Figure 1-17: The difficult part of the solution is to change directions as Indy descends between X2 and X4. He has to use a distant pole.

These solutions are due to TJ Takei.

Solution to Optimal Jargon

1. Suppose that in addition to the frequencies given in the warm-up, you know that in every message, B is always followed by A, and D is always followed by C. Could you arrive at a shorter encoding of the message?

In that case, we can form a code like this:

```
A−1
BA−01
C−000
DC−001
```

There will be 15 As by themselves with a cost of 15. There will be 15 BAs with a cost of 30. There will be 5 DCs with a cost of 15. There will be 5 Cs with a cost of 15.

So the total cost is only 75.

2. Suppose that in addition to the frequencies given in the warm-up, you know that in every message, D is always followed by C, C is always followed by B, and B is always followed by A. Could you arrive at an even shorter encoding of a 60-character message? Which phrases should be rendered as jargon?

This enables us to form the encoding:

```
A − 1
BA − 01
CBA − 000
DCBA − 001
```

In this case, there are 5 DCBAs with a cost of 15; 5 additional CBAs (i.e., not included in the DCBAs) with a cost of 15; 5 additional BAs with a cost of 10; and 15 additional As with a cost of 15. This gives a total of only 55 bits, less than one bit per character. The jargon terms should correspond to the phrases DCBA, CBA, BA, and A.

3. **Suppose that in addition to the frequencies given in the warm-up, you know that in every message, D is always followed by C, C is always followed by B, and B is followed by A 13 out of 15 times? What is the shortest encoding you could find of a 60-character message?**

We'll try two encodings. The first encoding includes the same phrases as in the solution to question 2, and then adds long codewords for the exceptional cases.

```
A − 1
BA − 01
CBA − 000
DCBA − 00101
DCB − 00100
CB − 00110
B − 00111
```

For this first encoding, let's consider two cases. In the first case, assume that there will be 5 DCBAs with a cost of 25; 5 additional CBAs (i.e., not included in the DCBAs) with a cost of 15; at least three additional BAs with a cost of 6; two Bs with a cost of 10; and 15 additional As with a cost of 15. In the second case, assume instead that, say, two of the CBAs were CBs instead, but that there were five BAs. The cost of the phrases beginning with C would then increase from 15 to 19, but the cost of the phrases beginning with B would decrease from 16 to 10. If two of the DCBAs were CDBs instead, then the cost of phrases beginning with D would not increase at all. So the worst kind of message from the point of this encoding is that two of the phrases that begin with B have no following A. The total cost of such a message is 25 + 15 + 6 + 10 + 15 = 71.

The second encoding uses only jargon terms having no exceptions:

```
A − 1
B − 01
CB − 000
DCB − 001
```

There will 5 DCBs with a cost of 15; 5 additional CBs (i.e., not included in the DCBs) with a cost of 15; five additional Bs with a cost of 10; and 30 As with a cost of 30. This gives a total of 15 + 15 + 10 + 30 = 70. Exceptions make jargon less attractive.

Solution to Using Your Marbles

1. On Tuesday, she again starts with 5 red marbles, 6 blue marbles, and 7 white ones. In order to make the bags more varied, she wants to pack the bags so that each bag differs by at least two "in-or-outs" from any other bag. An in-or-out consists of inserting a marble into a bag or removing a marble from a bag. So, for example, R and RR differ by only one in-or-out (insert R). On the other hand, RW and RB differ by two (remove W and insert B). How many different bags of marbles can Carol create that differ by at least two in-or-outs?

R, B, W, RBB, BWW, WWW, RBW, BRR; 8 altogether. The method here was to build up from small numbers. There could be no bags with two marbles because then they would differ from the singleton bags by just one marble.

2. On Wednesday, Carol is given a bag that she cannot open. She knows she has 18 marbles. She also knows that there is at least one red, at least one blue, and at least one white. Knowing only this information but before seeing the marbles, Carol receives a phone call. "Can you guarantee to be able to give each child a bag with a different collection of marbles (i.e., at least one in-or-out apart), if there are eight children at a party? If not, then can you make this guarantee if there are seven children? If so, then how about nine?" How should Carol answer?

If there is one R, one B and 16 Ws, then the best that Carol can do is to pack seven bags: W, R, B, WW, WWW, WWWW, WWWWW. The other W can be put either in a bag with a R or a B. Eight is not possible in this case because once there are only white marbles left, bags may differ only by number. If there are more than one red (or blue or both) marbles, but still fewer of these than white ones, then those red or blue marbles can be substituted for white ones in the larger bags. So Carol can guarantee at least seven bags, but no more.

3. On Thursday, she again knows only that she has 18 marbles and at least one of each color, and is in the same situation as Tuesday as far as wanting the children enjoy variety. So she wants each gift to differ from every other by at least two in-or-outs. How many children can she guarantee to prepare bags for in that case?

Again, if there is just one R, one B, and 16 whites, Carol can guarantee to prepare just six bags: W, R, B, WWW, WWWWW, WWWWWWW. She can't do better, because, once she gets to white marbles alone, the bags must differ by two marbles each.

4. On Friday, her friend Diane packs the bags. Diane assures Carol that (i) every bag contains a different (some difference of number in at least one color) collection of marbles, (ii) that there are 18 marbles to start with, (iii) there are more white than blue and more blue than red, and (iv) that the maximum different ones she could pack was seven. Assuming that Diane is an extremely capable packer, what is the maximum number of red marbles there could have been at the beginning?

If there is one red and two blues, this works: W, B, R WW, BW, WWW, WWWW.

There are not enough marbles left for a bag containing five white marbles. If there are two reds and three blues, then it is easy to form eight bags even without using all the marbles: W, B, R, WW, WB, WR, WWW, WBW.

If there are two reds and at least five blues (the maximum number of blues is seven because there must be more whites than blues), we could have at least eight bags, e.g., W,

B, R, WW, WB, WR, BB, WBW. Even more are possible, but by not specifying them, we handle more cases.

Similarly, if there are three reds and at least four blues, we could have at least eight bags, e.g., W, B, R, WW, WB, WR, BB, WRW.

Similar reasoning holds if there are four or five red marbles. Five is the upper limit of red marbles. There cannot be six or more red marbles, because then there would have to be at least seven blue marbles, leaving only five white ones.

Solution to Flipping Colors

1. **Can the knight flip the color of every square an odd number of times? If so, in how few moves?**

Steve Schaefer has found a 25 move solution which he describes as follows: "If we take the upper left corner to be square (0,0), then the first twenty moves flip the outer three rows/columns of the board, returning to the starting point at square (2,3). The four squares in the center of the board have not been flipped, and the starting square has been flipped twice. The remaining squares (2,3), (3,3), (3,4), (4,3), and (4,4) can be flipped with the following five moves":

```
(3,3), (4,3), (4,2)
(4,3), (4,4), (3,4)
(3,3), (3,2), (2,2)
(3,2), (4,2), (4,3)
(3,3), (2,3), (2,2)
```

With that introduction, we can now present Schaefer's 25-move solution, starting at (2,3):

```
 1: (1,3), (0,3), (0,2)
 2: (0,1), (0,0), (1,0)
 3: (1,1), (1,2), (2,2)
 4: (2,1), (2,0), (3,0)
 5: (3,1), (3,2), (4,2)
 6: (4,1), (4,0), (5,0)
 7: (6,0), (7,0), (7,1)
 8: (6,1), (5,1), (5,2)
 9: (6,2), (7,2), (7,3)
10: (6,3), (5,3), (5,4)
11: (6,4), (7,4), (7,5)
12: (7,6), (7,7), (6,7)
13: (6,6), (6,5), (5,5)
14: (5,6), (5,7), (4,7)
15: (4,6), (4,5), (3,5)
16: (3,6), (3,7), (2,7)
17: (1,7), (0,7), (0,6)
18: (1,6), (2,6), (2,5)
19: (1,5), (0,5), (0,4)
20: (1,4), (2,4), (2,3)
21: (3,3), (4,3), (4,2)
22: (4,3), (4,4), (3,4)
23: (3,3), (3,2), (2,2)
24: (3,2), (4,2), (4,3)
25: (3,3), (2,3), (2,2)
```

Solution to Scheduling Tradition

1. **Can you form an 11-day schedule for these teams that satisfies the constraints?**

This solution is from the classic puzzle book of Dudeney written a century ago. The pairs for each day are separated by spaces. You'll see that except for the A column, all other columns are different rotations of BEGFKHICDLJ, a sequence of letters in which all the non-A letters appear exactly once. Consider some letter, say E. By construction, E is in each one of the non-A columns exactly once. Therefore E plays against A. Also, by construction, E is in a given day's row exactly once (because all the rotations differ).

> day 1: AB CD EF GH IJ KL
>
> day 2: AE DL GK FI CB HJ
>
> day 3: AG LJ FH KC DE IB
>
> day 4: AF JB KI HD LG CE
>
> day 5: AK BE HC IL JF DG
>
> day 6: AH EG ID CJ BK LF
>
> day 7: AI GF CL DB EH JK
>
> day 8: AC FK DJ LE GI BH
>
> day 9: AD KH LB JG FC EI
>
> day 10: AL HI JE BF KD GC
>
> day 11: AJ IC BG EK HL FD

How do we know that E encounters every other letter? In every pair of columns, except the leftmost, E encounters two teams. We just have to ensure that the teams in question are different every time. This is the case because if we list the pairs of columns by the offset from the first letter in the sequence BEGFKHICDLJ, then we see that the column paired with A begins at B, so is at an offset of 0. The next pair begins with C and D respectively at offsets 7 and 8, so their offsets differ by 1. We'll denote that fact by the sentence "CD are at offsets 7 and 8, so the offsets differ by 1."

> CD are at offsets 7 and 8, so the offsets differ by 1
>
> EF are at offsets 1 and 3, so the offsets differ by 2
>
> GH are at offsets 2 and 5, so the offsets differ by 3
>
> IJ are at offsets 6 and 10, so the offsets differ by 4
>
> KL are at offsets 4 and 9, so the offsets differ by 5

Because the various column pairs differ by different offsets, a given pair XY will meet in only one column pair. For example, E and B will meet in the column pair with offset 1, as will E and G. E and F as well as E and J will meet in the column pair with offset 2 and so on. Whereas we have used E as an example, the same reasoning holds for all letters B to L. The case of A is clear by inspection of the first two columns.

Solution to Fractal Biology

1. Can you achieve the wounded distance two condition for eight nodes using 16 links, assuming no node can have more than four interaction links?

With eight nodes, one needs only 16 links, as demonstrated in Figure 1-18.

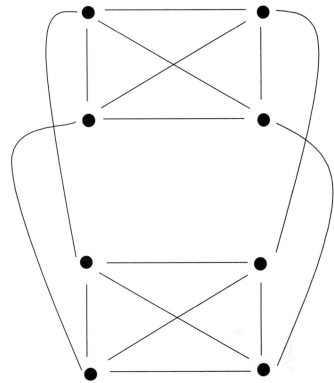

Figure 1-18: An eight-node network in which there is a two-link path from any node to any other even if a node is deleted. Within one foursome, there is a single link from any node to any other. For a trip from a node n in one foursome to a node m in the other foursome, there are two paths of length at most two. These go through different intermediate nodes.

2. What is the fewest number of links needed to achieve the wounded distance two condition for 12 nodes and at most five interaction links for any node?

With 12 nodes, one could design three sets of four nodes that are completely connected (requiring $3 \times 6 = 18$ nodes) and then add in four links between every pair of four, leading to an additional 12 links for a total of 30 altogether.

3. What is the fewest number of links needed for 12 nodes, but without any limit on the number of interaction links any particular node can have?

If there is no limit on the number of links per protein node, try the design of Figure 1-19. You would need only 21 links. This is called the two-fan design, because each hub creates a fan. One needs two fans in case one hub is wounded.

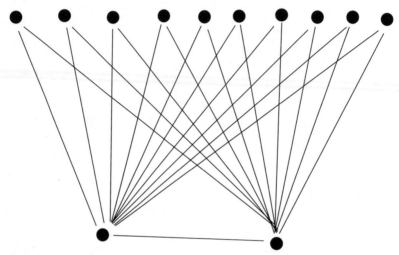

Figure 1-19: A twelve node, wounded distance two network using only 21 links.

4. We have a particular network having 108 proteins. We don't yet know all the interactions. What is the fewest number of links needed to achieve the wounded distance two condition for any pair among these 108 nodes if there is a limit of 60 interactions that any single node can have? Try for a solution that uses fewer than 600 links.

Divide the nodes into 96 nodes (the base nodes) and 12 other nodes that will perform a connection function (the switchboard nodes). Number the 96 base nodes from 1 to 96. Call 1 through 24 the A nodes, 25 through 48 the B nodes, 49 through 72 the C nodes, and 73 through 96 the D nodes.

A good way to conceptualize the problem is that each base node group forms the supervertex of a tetrahedron (large black circles). Along each of the six edges linking supervertices there are two "switchboard" nodes, as you can see in Figure 1-20.

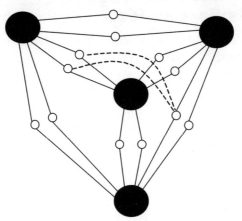

Figure 1-20: Switchboard nodes are clear circles. Supervertices, each consisting of 24 nodes, are big dark circles. The basic design represents 576 links. In addition, we have shown two links (the dashed curves) between non-neighboring switchboard nodes. Altogether there are 12 such links.

Each switchboard node is connected to every node in the two supervertices that form its edge (2×24 links). Thus, the total number of links involving base nodes is $2 \times 2 \times 24 \times 6 = 576$. Two switchboard nodes are "neighbors" if they share a supervertex. Each switchboard node needs a direct link to non-neighbors only. Each switchboard is the neighbor to all but two of the other switchboards. Linking to those non-neighbors adds a total of $12 \times 2 = 24$ to the collective degree of the switchboard nodes. This translates to half that number of edges, for a total of 12. This yields a total of $588 = 576 + 12$ links.

This solution is due to TJ Takei.

> *Note: The network problems here fit a general formulation: Find the minimum number of links necessary for N nodes, maximum distance D between any pair of unwounded nodes where the maximum degree (number of interactions per node) K, and there may be up to X wounded nodes. Such questions might bear distinct relevance to biology. Here are two mathematical biology papers on similar topics that I like very much:*
>
> *"Regulation of metabolic networks: understanding metabolic complexity in the systems biology era," Lee Sweetlove and Alisdair Fernie, New Phytologist 2005, 168: 9-24.*
>
> *"Evolutionary capacitance as a general feature of complex gene networks," Aviv Bergman and Mark Siegal, Nature 2003 Jul 31; 424(6948): 549-52.*

Solution to As Easy as Pie

1. Find a cut design obeying the above three rules that minimizes the total length of the perimeters for five pieces.

Make the first cut with a width of 1/5 of the total, and the second cut perpendicularly with a width of 1/4. Repeat the process with ever-wider widths (4/15 and 3/8) to keep the same area until the last cut halves the remaining piece (see Figure 1-21). This gives a total perimeter of 10 1/6 or about 10.17.

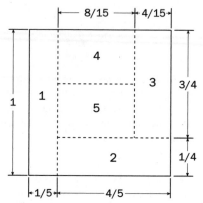

Figure 1-21: Recursive perpendicular cuts satisfying the child cut rule.

2. How much better can you do for five pieces, after dropping the child cut rule?

The best design for five pieces using cuts that are parallel to the edges of the original square is shown in Figure 1-22. Rectangles 1, 2, 3, and 4 all have dimensions b by 1-b (having an area of 1/5). This gives a total perimeter of $4(2 + 1/\sqrt{5})$, which is about 9.8.

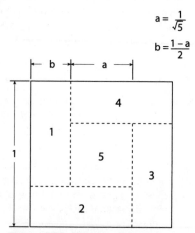

Figure 1-22: Without the child cut rule, one can obtain a smaller total perimeter for five pieces.

3. What about nine pieces?

For nine pieces without the child-cut rule, we get the similar design in Figure 1-23. This gives a perimeter of about 15.3.

$$a_2 = \frac{\sqrt{5}}{3}$$

$$a_1 = \frac{1}{3}$$

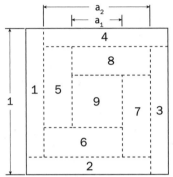

Figure 1-23: Without the child cut rule, here is the best design I know of for nine pieces.

4. Can you get a smaller perimeter for five pieces, if, in addition to dropping the child cut rule, you drop the rule that cuts must be parallel to the original sides?

A beautifully economical design for five pieces without the child cut rule that permits cuts at an angle to the original edges is shown in Figure 1-24. The slant is about 19 degrees from the horizontal. This gives a total perimeter of under 9.4.

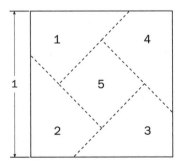

Figure 1-24: Without the child cut rule or the requirement that all cuts must be parallel to an original side, one can reduce the perimeter quite noticeably.

TJ Takei provided these solutions, the best I know of for these problems. For the tilting calculation of question 4, he used Gnu Octave.

Solution to Lucky Roulette

1.   **Do you ask for a spin of the chamber before the third trigger pull? How about before the fourth trigger pull? Using your best strategy, what are your chances of survival ignoring the first trigger pull?**

If you don't have me spin again now, you have a 1 in 3 chance of dying in the third pull of the trigger, which is the same as if you ask me to spin. But the advantage of spinning is that if I spin now and you survive the third trigger pull, then you will return to the 1 in 4 chance of dying for the last trigger pull.

Using that strategy (don't spin before the second trigger pull, spin before the third, and don't spin before the fourth), your chances of survival beyond the first trigger pull are $3/4 \times 2/3 \times 3/4 = 3/8$. If you had asked me to spin every time, your chances of survival would be only 8/27, a little less than 1/3. Sorry for the violent setting, but I hope it helped focus your mind.

Solution to Legal Logic

1.   **If each patient has a 0.005 probability of being hurt, how likely is it to get one failure within the first 50 patients?**

As preparation for our later work, write a procedure using a random number generator that produces a 1 with a probability of 0.005 and a 0 otherwise for 50 times. Count the number of 1s. Call this procedure 10,000 times. You can see that there will be one failure in the first 50 patients approximately 22% of the time. This result can also be obtained analytically: probability of at least one failure = 1 - probability of no failures in 50 = 1 - (1 - probability of failure each time)^{50} = 1 - (0.995^{50}) = 0.222.

2.   **Suppose that 18 people out of 4,000 have been hurt by the device. There are eight hospitals, each of which has treated 500 patients. What is the likelihood that at least one hospital exceeds a 1% test, i.e., has 6 patients who were hurt, even if the underlying chance of failure were in fact independent of hospital and is 0.005 per patient?**

To solve this question empirically, create groups corresponding to 1 to 500 inclusive, 501 to 1,000 inclusive, ..., 3,501 to 4,000 inclusive. Do the following 10,000 times: Take the 18 numbers uniformly at random without replacement (i.e., never take the same one again) over the range of 1 to 4,000. See if any group has more than 1% failures. You will see that between 14% and 15% of the time, at least one group does. This again is a false guilty rate.

3. Suppose the distribution of patients were much more skewed, with seven hospitals having treated only 200 patients each and the remaining one having treated all the rest. How likely is it that at least one of those smaller hospitals had hurt three people or more under the same conditions (i.e., 18 people who were hurt overall and the underlying chance of failure is 0.005 per patient)?

In this case, the tort lawyers will win around 35% of the time. The method is similar to the method we used to answer question 2 except the groups correspond to 1 to 200 inclusive, 201 to 400 inclusive, ..., 1,201 to 1,400 inclusive, and then 1,401 to 4,000.

4. Suppose we say that if a single hospital has more than 2% of bad outcomes, then that is a bad hospital. Assume that each hospital treats 500 patients. What is the likelihood for at least one hospital to hurt 10 or more people if the 0.005 hurt probability held and there were no bias in any hospital?

This would happen only about 5 times out of 10,000. This is so unlikely that there is a good chance the hospital really is bad.

5. How would you answer the last question in the case that seven hospitals each treat only 200 patients and one treats 3,600?

In this case, the probability increases to about 2.5% (250 times out of 10,000). I'd still avoid that hospital.

Solution to The Box Chip Game

1. For four chips and two guesses per color, can you figure out a way to win at least 1/6 of the time, assuming all rearrangements are equally likely?

Black guess: 1, 2

White guess: 1, 2

Red guess: 3, 4

Green guess: 3, 4

You win 4 times out of the 24 (= 4!) possible permutations. Why 4? Because black and white can be in either order among the first two boxes; red and green can be in either order among the last two boxes. Because 4 out of 24 is 1/6, you win 1/6 of the time. I think that's the best one can do. If you can show me wrong, then please let me know.

2. What if there are six chips and three guesses per color?

For six chips with three guesses per color, the best is 1/20. As puzzlist Alan Dragoo puts it: "Guess the same half of the boxes for one half of the chip colors and the other half of the boxes for the other half of the chips. This gives a probability of $(n/2)! \times (n/2)! / n!$ of winning." For 6, this comes out to be $3! \times 3!/6! = 36/720 = 1/20$.

3. **How does this probability generalize for n chips (n even) and n/2 guesses per color?**

Following Alan Dragoo's suggestion is the best approach I know of. It works for all even numbers, which is fine because the puzzle allows only even numbers. Unfortunately, $(n/2)! \times (n/2)! / n!$ rapidly approaches zero. For 8, it's only 1.4%. For 12, it's 0.1%.

4. **How well can you do in the case of four chips and two guesses under the procedural agent assumption? (Hint: You can win over 40 percent of the time.)**

Identify the colors with numbers. This is an arbitrary association, but fixing it consistently will help.

> Black — 1
>
> White — 2
>
> Red — 3
>
> Green — 4

Here are the programs. The boxes are numbered 1, 2, 3, and 4 in left-to-right order.

> Black: 1; Black→win, White→2, Red→3, Green→4
>
> White: 2; White→win, Black→1, Red→3, Green→4
>
> Red: 3; Red→win, Black→1, White→2, Green→4
>
> Green: 4; Green→win, Black→1, White→2, Red→3

The notation means the following: Black (the agent associated with the black chip) starts at box 1; if box 1 has a black chip, then Black wins; if box 1 has a white chip, then Black next opens box 2; if box 1 has a red chip, then Black next opens box 3; and so on. Suppose box 1 has a white chip, so Black opens box 2. If box 2 then has a green chip, then Black next opens box 4.

This strategy wins in 10 out of the 24 possible permutations. To see why, consider any ordering of the colors in boxes.

1	2	3	4	win/lose
Black	White	Red	Green	win
Black	White	Green	Red	win
Black	Red	White	Green	win
Black	Red	Green	White	lose
Black	Green	White	Red	lose
Black	Green	Red	White	win
White	Black	Red	Green	win
White	Black	Green	Red	win
White	Red	Black	Green	lose
White	Red	Green	Black	lose
White	Green	Black	Red	lose
White	Green	Red	Black	lose
Red	Black	White	Green	lose
Red	Black	Green	White	lose
Red	White	Black	Green	win
Red	White	Green	Black	lose
Red	Green	Black	White	win
Red	Green	White	Black	lose
Green	Black	White	Red	lose
Green	Black	Red	White	lose
Green	White	Black	Red	lose
Green	White	Red	Black	win
Green	Red	Black	White	lose
Green	Red	White	Black	win

Notice that there are 10 wins here.

5. **How well can you do if you have six chips and three guesses?**

Out of the 720 possible permutations of the 6 elements, you can win 276 times (or more than 38 percent of the time). The agents all agree in advance on the following arbitrary association A of boxes to colors. These indicate which box next to pick based on the color found in the previous box.

Black→box 1

White→box 2

Red→box 3

Green→box 4

Blue→box 5

Orange→box 6

Here is the program for the agent corresponding to color X. Start at the box corresponding to color X in association A. If you find X, then you've won, so you can stop. Otherwise, look up the color you find, say Y, in A and look at that box. If you find X, then you've won, so you can stop. Otherwise, look up the color you find, say Z, in A and look at that box. If you find X, then you've won. Otherwise, you lose.

For example, White does the following:

White: 2; Black→1, White→win, Red→3, Green→4, Blue→5, Orange→6;

Note: I first heard this puzzle from Peter Winkler. Michael Rabin explained the procedural agent idea to me. What is truly fascinating about this problem is the use of arbitrary assignments. In this, as well as in several other puzzles described or invented by Winkler, the idea is to commit everything to one approach. You either win all the time or lose often — kind of a start-up mentality.

By the way, if you happen to be an algebraist, characterizing when the contestant wins can be expressed succinctly: You win whenever the colors arranged in the boxes guarantee that the longest cycle in the arbitrary permutation is of length n/2 or less. Let me explain. First, notice that the mapping from colors to numbers is a permutation (a rearrangement) of those colors. For example,

Black→box 1

White→box 2

says that Black should be put first in the list, White should be put second, and so on. We don't move the chips, of course, but it is in this way that we can think of these assignments as a permutation. Now, a cycle occurs when following the box colors happens to return us to a box we've already visited.

Suppose, for example, that the six boxes have the following colors:

1: Blue

2: Black

3: Red

4: Orange

5: White

6: Green

and we use the arbitrary permutation:

Black→box 1

White→box 2

Red→box 3

Green→box 4

Blue→box 5

Orange→box 6

Suppose we are looking for Red. The permutation says to go to box 3. As it happens, we find Red in box 3. So the length of the Red cycle is one. Suppose we are looking for Black.

The permutation says to look in box 1.

We find Blue.

So the permutation says to look at box 5.

We find White.

So the permutation says to look at box 2.

We find Black.

At this point we win, but note that the next block to look at would be box 1. That is, the color of the chip that sends us back to the first box we looked at must be the color we are looking for. (For Black, we first look at box 1 and the color of the chip in box 2 would send us back to box 1.) In this case, the cycle in the permutation is of length three $1→5→2→1$. In fact, for this permutation, every cycle is of length three or less.

On the other hand, suppose that the arrangement of the colors in the boxes were:

1: Blue

2: Black

3: Red

4: White

5: Orange

6: Green

Now consider starting with White using the same permutation as above:

> Start in box 2.
>
> Find Black.
>
> Go to box 1.
>
> Find Blue.
>
> Go to box 5.
>
> Find Orange.
>
> Go to box 6.
>
> Find Green.
>
> Go to box 4.
>
> Find White.

In this case, we have 2→1→5→6→4→2. This is a cycle of length five.

Moral of the story: A succinct statement of the solution may not lead to a succinct explanation of the statement.

Solution to Feedback Dividends

1.   If Pgood is 0.9, what is the probability of hitting row 8, column 5 using the FeedYes strategy and using the FeedNo strategy?

The probability of winning under FeedYes is about 0.89 when Pgood is 0.9. It cannot be better than 0.9 because if you are on the second from top row and adjacent to the winning square, there is some chance of losing. The strategy for FeedYes consists of trying to reduce the horizontal distance to the goal to zero (or to one on rows that are an odd distance away). Calculating the probability involves the following key recurrence ideas: If you are n steps (n > 0) away from the top row and 0 distance away, then your probability of hitting is the same as the probability of hitting if you are n-1 steps away and one away from column 5. Otherwise, with probability Pgood you will be one column closer to your goal and with probability 1-Pgood you will be one farther from the goal, both with n-1 steps.

Under the FeedNo strategy, the probability is about 0.55 when Pgood is 0.9. To compute the probability for FeedNo, assume a strategy that will take four aims to the right and three aims to the left since this gives the best likelihood of hitting the destination. Given this, there are four ways to win: All seven aims are true; three of the right aims are true and two of the left are; two of the right are true and one of the left; and one right and zero left.

So, the feedback dividend is about 1.6.

2.   For which value of Pgood does the feedback dividend reach its greatest value? What is the feedback dividend in that case?

The value of Pgood for which the dividend ratio is highest is not 0.75 as one might think, but something around 0.772. For that value, the dividend ratio reaches 1.99.

3. If we cut off the three rightmost columns and the two leftmost columns, then which value of Pgood would give the highest feedback dividend? Assume that falling off the board gives a certain loss.

In both the FeedNo and FeedYes cases, the analysis combines short trips: One wants to go from row 1, column 4 to row 3, column 4 in the first two moves, then to row 5, column 4 in the second two moves, then row 7, column 4, and finally row 8, column 5. For FeedNo, this gives a formula like the following:

$$(((Pgood^2) + ((1-Pgood)^2))^3) \times Pgood.$$

For FeedYes, this gives a formula that is $Pgood^4$.

This gives a maximum feedback dividend of 1.75 when Pgood is 0.71.

Alan Dragoo contributed greatly to these solutions.

> *Note: I have a friend who likes to swim backstroke in swimming pools that have no lane markers. He admits to colliding with other people a lot.*

Solution to Number Clues

1. For the first p, q pair, lcm(p,q) = 60, p × q = 240. What are p and q?

Here are the possible ways for two numbers to divide 240 and satisfy the lcm constraint.

4, 60 — No good because p and q must both be two digit numbers.

12, 20 — This could work.

So the solution must be 12, 20.

2. The product of p and q is 140. gcd(p,q) = 2. What are p and q?

The factors of 140 are 2, 2, 5, and 7. Both p and q have 2 as a factor. So, the possible values of p and q are:

2, 70 — No good because p and q must both be two digit numbers.

4, 35 — No good for same reason.

10, 14 — Possible.

3. There is a pair p and q whose lcm(p,q) = 35. What are p and q?

Because lcm(p,q) = 35, at least one of p and q must have one 5 and at least one must have one 7. To satisfy the two-digit requirement, they both must. So p = q = 35.

4. The sequence of numbers that opens the safe is a permutation of five numbers from the hints. The sequence enjoys the following property: The greatest common divisors between neighbors of the sequence strictly increase as one proceeds from left to right in the sequence, but all greatest common divisors are single digits. What is the sequence that opens the safe?

The numbers that open the safe are: 10 12 20 35 14. The greatest common divisor between 10 and 12 is 2; the greatest common divisor between 12 and 20 is 4; between 20 and 35 is 5; and between 35 and 14 is 7.

Solution to Mind Games

1. What is the smallest number of bit questions sufficient to determine a five-bit sequence no matter what it is? Remember that none of your bit questions need be correct. You just need to know how to crack the secret at the end.

Five are sufficient, even if all answers come at the end. Here are the guesses:

10000

11000

11100

11110

11111

Here's why this is enough. Number the positions from left to right at 1, 2, 3, 4, and 5. Consider position i. Suppose that there is a 1 in position i, for i > 1. Then the number correct will increase by one in the reported answers of the ith bit question compared to the previous 1. For example, suppose the fourth position has a 1. That is, the secret code has the form xxx1x. Then 11110 will have a number count that is one higher than 11100. Conversely, if the fourth position has a 0, then 11110 will have a number count that is one less than 11100.

So far, we know about all bit positions except i = 1. We can determine the value of that bit position by examining the number correct for 10000. For example, if the last four digits are 0110, then the secret code is either 00110 or 10110. If the secret code were 00110, then the first bit question (10000) would yield a number correct of 2. If the secret code were 10110, then the number correct would be 3.

It turns out that four questions are enough also. Make the first two questions be 00000 and 11100. In most cases, this narrows down the bit sequences quite substantially. For example, if the answers to these first two questions are 4 and 1, respectively, then the remaining possibilities are: 00001 and 00010. So we will focus on the two difficult situations where there are six possibilities left. Those situations occur when the answers to the first two questions are either 2 and 3 respectively or 3 and 2 respectively. Suppose the answers to the first two questions are 2 and 3 respectively. Then the remaining possibilities are:

01101

01110

10101

10110

11001

11010

Let's say we ask 01110, a codeword that differs by at least two bits from both of the first questions. This will give us the following possible answers:

0 — impossible

1 — remaining possibilities: 10101 and 11001

2 — impossible

3 — remaining possibilities 01101, 10110, and 11010

4 — impossible

5 — remaining possibility 01110

The only difficult case is the one where the remaining possibilities are 01101, 10110, and 11010. In this case, we guess 00101. There are only three possible answers, each of which leads to a unique conclusion.

0 — 11010

2 — 10110

4 — 01101

Philip Daniel Rogers suggested this approach to a solution. There is no elegant closed form proof that this always works and the program is a bit complex. However, the program for the case when there is no feedback is quite simple, as you'll see next.

2. **Suppose we change the game to make it a little more difficult: You ask some number of questions and then I answer them all after you have asked all your questions. In that case, how many bit questions are sufficient?**

Surprisingly, the very same guesses used in question 1 give a unique "signature" for each possible secret. That is, you make the following guesses:

00000

11100

01110

00101

Each possible sequence of five bits will give four answers and those answers differ for any pair of sequences. For example, suppose 11001 is the secret. That secret yields an answer of 2 correct to the bit question 00000, 3 to the bit question 11100, 1 to the bit question 01110, and 2 to the bit question 00101. No other bit sequence produces this same signature of answers: 2 3 1 2. Thus, you make the above four guesses, look at the signature, and determine which is the secret bit sequence. Writing a program to compute the signature given a series of guesses is, of course, very easy.

3. Given that the low info answers come at the end and there is no answer at all to the first bit question, is it possible to find the secret number, no matter what it is? If so, how many bit questions (counting the first one) do you need to pose in order to guarantee finding the secret number?

If, after the first guess, you are told only whether the number of correct ones has increased or decreased and all these answers come at the end, then six bit guesses suffice to know the secret code. Start with 00000.

00000

10000

11000

11100

11110

11111

You can determine whether each bit position is 1 or 0 by whether the number correct has increased or decreased relative to the previous one.

4. How many bit questions do you need, if you hear the low info answers immediately after posing them?

If the answers are given immediately after they are asked, Tom Rokicki suggests the following approach requiring only five questions altogether. The basic idea is to use the fact that three answers are possible (same (S), increase (+), or decrease (-)) whereas our method for the previous question used only + and -. Start with 00000 again. Next guess 3 (that is 00011 in binary). This changes two bits, so if the answer is S (same number correct), then one of these 1s is correct and one isn't. On the other hand, if the answer is + (increase), then both must be correct. Similarly, if the answer is -. Continue with this reasoning and you'll find the answer. If you get stuck, see the following:

```
[3,
   S:[29,
      SS:[4,
            SS+:[14,
                  SS+-:{5},
                  SS+S:{22},
                  SS++:{14}],
            SS-:[14,
                  SS--:{17},
                  SS-+:{26},
                  SS-S:{9}]],
         S-:[5,
            S-S:{10,18},
            S-+:[10,
                  S-+S:{6},
                  S-++:{2},
                  S-+-:{1}]],
         S+:[5,
            S+S:{13,21},
            S+-:[10,
                  S+-+:{30},
                  S+--:{29},
                  S+-S:{25}]]],
   -:[5,
      -S:[9,
         -SS:{0,16},
         -S+:{8,24}],
      -+:[8,
         -+-:{4,20},
         -++:{12,28}]],
   +:[5,
      +-:[8,
         +-+:{11,27},
         +--:{3,19}],
      +S:[9,
         +SS:{15,31},
         +S-:{7,23}]]]
```

The answers to the left of the colon are the previous answers. The indentation gives precedence. For example, +:[5 means "if the answer to the first question is +, then ask about 5 (00101)."

5. How does this generalize if the code is N digits long, but the digits could be base b for some b > 2? For example, b could be 10 and all digits 0 through 9 would be allowed. I have a solution when all answers come at the end, but that requires 1 + (b-1) × N questions. I don't think it's optimal.

We can use the reasoning of question 3. Here are the first questions to find a secret that is base 10.

00000

10000

20000

30000

40000

50000

60000

70000

80000

90000

01000

02000

03000

04000

05000

06000

07000

08000

09000

This yields a set of questions of size $1 + N(b-1)$, but I await a clever reader to suggest a better approach.

Solution to Refuse and Reveal

1. Rosalba: "I have five integers that may or may not be distinct."

   Quentin: "What is the minimum?"

   Rosalba: "20."

   Quentin: "Which of these would not allow me to infer all their values: number distinct, mean, maximum, or median?"

   Rosalba: "Only the median."

   Quentin: "Great. I know the numbers."

   What are they?

They must all be 20. Any of the other statistics would reveal this fact for sure.

2.   Rosalba: "I have seven integers that may or may not be distinct."

Quentin: "What is the minimum?"

Rosalba: "20."

Quentin: "Which of these are you willing to tell me (i.e., would not allow me to infer all their values): mean, median, and maximum?"

Rosalba: "All of them."

Quentin: "Ok, what is the maximum?"

Rosalba: "21."

Quentin: "I know which of mean and median you're willing to tell me now."

Which? Why?

The mean would be enough to determine how many 20s and how many 21s there are. For example, if there are four 20s and three 21s, then the mean would be about 20.43. Knowing the median would not be enough because a median of 20, for example, could result from a situation in which there are three 20s and four 21s or five 20s and two 21s.

3.   Rosalba: "Can you find some situation in which I would be happier to tell you the mean rather than the median?"

Quentin: "Could you give me a hint?"

Rosalba: "In an example I can think of, there are three numbers, two of them distinct." Give it a try.

Suppose there are three numbers and two distinct ones. If you know that the minimum is 20 and the median is 23, then you know that the other number is also 23. On the other hand if you know that the mean is 22, for example, this could result from 20, 20, and 26.

4.   Rosalba: "Can you find some situation in which all of minimum, maximum, mean, and median are necessary and sufficient to find the identities of five numbers that are all integers?"

Minimum is 20, maximum is 22. Mean is 21.2. This could be explained by three 22s and two 20s or by two 22s, two 21s, and one 20. The median will tell you which.

5.   Rosalba: "There are 17 numbers that are not all distinct. Their minimum is 30, mean is 34, and median is 35."

Quentin: "What is their total distance to 35?"

Rosalba: "I won't tell you, but the total distance to 35 is five less than the total distance to 38. Whoops! I shouldn't have told you that."

Quentin laughing: "You're right. Now I know the numbers."

What are they?

The point to which the total distance is guaranteed to be at a minimum is the median. That is, if there are an odd number n of values altogether, then the sum of the distances to the median is smaller than to any other point. Here is why. Suppose the median is m. Let the total distance to m be x. Now consider the total distance to m+1. Because m is a median, there are (n-1)/2 values that are m or less. So, at least 1+(n-1)/2 values increase their distance by 1 when calculating the total distance to m+1, including the median again. At most (n-1)/2 values decrease their distance by at most 1 when calculating the total distance to m+1.

So if there are 17 numbers and the median is 35, the mean is 34 and the distance to 38 is x+5, then there is one instance of 35, no instances of 36, and one instance of 37. Here is why: If there were one instance of 35, zero instances of 36 and 37, then the distance to 38 would increase by $3 \times 8 = 24$ for the numbers below 35 and decrease by 3×8 for the numbers greater than or equal to 38. The distance for 35 itself would increase by 3. This would give a net increase of 3. The fact that there is a net increase of 4 must mean that there is an instance of 37. In this case the net decrease for the upper eight values would be $3 \times 7 = 21$ for those greater than or equal to 38 and 1 for 37. This implies that there are seven values that are 38 or greater and one 35 and one 37. Because the mean is 34, the total distance to the mean of the numbers greater than the mean is at least $1 + 3 + 28$; we get those numbers from the 35, the 37, and the seven values that are 38 or greater. This total is 32. The values below the mean must match this, so they must all be 30s. Since they cannot be less than 30, the uppermost value cannot be greater than 38. So there are eight 30s, one 35, one 37, and seven 38s.

6. **How would your answer to this question change if there were 1701 numbers but otherwise the same information as in the previous question?**

The reasoning is exactly the same as for 17 numbers with one 35, one 37, 849 38s, and 850 30s.

Tom Rokicki helped greatly to clarify the formulation of this puzzle.

Solution to A Biting Maze

1. **The challenge is to find a route to the final page, and to decrypt the words and phrases on the way. There are hints in the encrypted words (they form a sentence of natural poetry) and in other parts of the Web page. Give it a try.**

Here is a list of the page ids along with the decryption of the words and phrases in those pages.

f42, if

f37, you

f33, would

f32, see

f39, all

f44, of

f28, nature

f52, gathered

f23, up

f51, at

f17, one

f13, point

f46, in

f53, all

f34, her

f29, loveliness

f14, and

f19, her

f36, skill

f0, and

f2, her

f30, deadliness

f16, and

f4, her

f10, sex

f49, where

f15, would

f31, you

f3, find

f12, a

f27, more

f7, exquisite

f8, symbol

f22, than

f9, the

f6, mosquito

f25, if you have found the whole route to get here, you have solved the maze. congratulations.

The great natural biologist Havelock Ellis wrote this sentence in 1920. Take a look before you squash the next bug.

Solution to Mad Mix

1. We want a mixture having 2.7 liters of supertox in a three-liter mixture. We don't want to pour more than 10 liters of any liquid laced with supertox down the drain. How can we achieve this?

First obtain 9 liters of supertox in the 10-vessel. (Fill the 10-vessel with supertox, pour the result into the 7-vessel until it fills, empty the 7-vessel into the reservoir, and then pour the three remaining in the 10-vessel into the 7-vessel. Now fill the 10-vessel again with supertox and fill the 7-vessel, which takes only 4 liters (since it already has 3). So the 10-vessel has 6 liters. Empty the 7-vessel into the supertox reservoir and pour the 6 liters from the 10-vessel into the 7-vessel. Now, fill the 10-vessel with supertox again. Pour into the 7-vessel until it is full, leaving 9 liters of supertox in the 10-vessel.) Then add one liter of water to the 10-vessel. Pour this mixture into the 7-vessel, leaving 3 liters in the 10-vessel having 2.7 liters of supertox.

2. Can we get a mixture that is 2/9 supertox and the rest water without pouring any supertox down the drain?

First obtain 2 liters of supertox in the 10-vessel. To obtain 2 liters of supertox in the 10-vessel, fill the 7-vessel with supertox, and empty it into the 10. Repeat; but now there are 4 liters left in the 7-vessel. Return the 10 liters to the supertox reservoir. Now pour the 4 liters into the 10-vessel and refill the 7-vessel with supertox. Now pour from the 7-liter vessel to the 10. When you are done, there will be 1 liter left in the 7-vessel. Empty the 10-vessel back into the reservoir and then transfer the single liter from the 7-vessel to the 10-vessel. Fill the 7-vessel from the reservoir and pour into the 10-vessel, leaving space for two. Fill the 7-vessel again from the supertox reservoir and pour into the 10-vessel. This fills the 10-vessel and leaves 5 in the 7-vessel. Empty the 10-vessel back into the supertox reservoir and pour the 5 from the 7-vessel to the 10-vessel. Refill the 7-vessel. Pour from the 7-vessel into the 10-vessel, leaving two liters in the 7-vessel. Empty the 10-vessel back into the supertox reservoir and then pour the two liters from the 7-vessel to the 10-vessel. Finally, fill the 7-vessel with water and pour that into the 10-vessel.

3. Can we get a 26% concentration of supertox in the 7-liter container?

With a big extra bucket, one can obtain any mixture satisfying a ratio $p/(p+q)$ of supertox where p and q are whole numbers whose sum is 100 or less. Here's what you do: Create p liters of supertox and dump them into the big extra bucket and then q liters of water and dump. Now you have that ratio. Suppose you want 53 liters, for example. You fill the 10-liter vessel five times and put the results in the big bucket. Now fill the 10-liter vessel one more time, pour into the 7-liter vessel. The three liters left over go into the big bucket. So, in this case, we want a mixture of 10 liters or more having a concentration of 26% of supertox. So, if we had 13 liters of supertox and 37 liters of water, that would do it. Fill the 10-liter vessel with supertox; pour into the big bucket. Fill the 10-liter vessel with supertox and pour it into the 7-liter vessel. The 3 remaining liters go into the big bucket. Empty the 7-liter vessel into the supertox reservoir. Obtaining 37 liters of water is easy, of course (three 10s and a 7). Once you have the mixture, fill the 10-liter vessel. There will be 2.6 liters of supertox in there.

This solution is due to Vlad Simionescu.

4. Suppose that we want to get mixtures that are all supertox, 1/2 supertox, 1/3 supertox, 1/4 supertox, ... 1/50 supertox. You are allowed to specify the size of the two vessels. You may even include fractional sizes as long as the smallest vessel contains at least one liter and the largest contains at most 30 liters. In addition, you have the big bucket again with capacity over 100 liters. Which two vessel sizes would you choose in order to obtain each of these mixtures? Given those vessel sizes and given a target mixture, how would you obtain it?

Suppose we want all fractions up to $1/k$. In our case, $k = 50$. Let the basic unit be 0.6 liters and then the smaller bucket can be 17 basic units or 10.2 liters, and the larger bucket can be 50 basic units or 30 liters. Because 17 is a prime number, we can generate any number k of units between 1 and 49 from these even without the extra bucket. Start by generating 1 unit of supertox and putting it in the big bucket (which can be very small in fact). Then generate k units of water and mix.

This extremely elegant solution is due to Ivan Rezanka. Ivan has shown how to solve this problem without the extra bucket. The basic hint is to put an amount of supertox in the large vessel such that when the vessel is subsequently filled to completion with water, the desired concentration is achieved. This can be done if the larger vessel is viewed as consisting of L units where L is the least common multiple of numbers 2, 3, ..., k.

Solution to Dig That!

In these solutions, call the north-south roads columns and the east-west roads rows. The center line is column 4 between Start and End.

1. If the tunnel is at most eight blocks long and begins at Start and ends at End, then what is the minimum number of probe devices you would need to guarantee to determine the precise route of the tunnel in one hour?

Because the straight line road from Start to End is of length six, the most the tunnel can deviate from the center line is by one. For this reason, place probes one away from the center line at the intersections indicated by the circles in Figure 1-25.

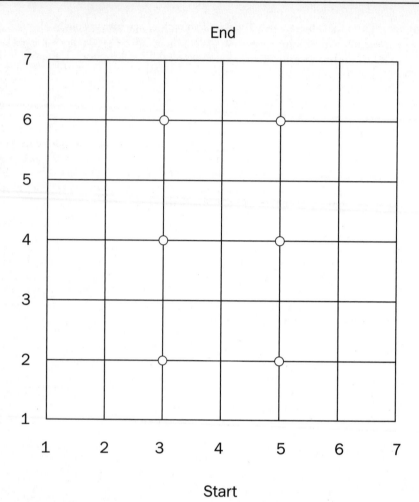

Figure 1-25: Because you know the direction of the roads as they leave an intersection, each pair on each row determines the fate of the tunnel on that row and the next.

Here is the reasoning. If no probe detects a tunnel, then the tunnel goes north up the center. It has no choice, because there are no loops. If a tunnel goes through a probe (represented by a circle), we can tell whether it is coming from the south and whether it is going north, west, or east. For example, if neither probe at row 2 detects the tunnel, then the tunnel must go north up the center at least till east-west cross street 3. By contrast, if the tunnel approaches the probe at row 2, column 5 from the west and leaves going north, then we know the following: The tunnel went north from Start one block, then turned east one block (where it encounters the probe), then turned north one block (to arrive at column 5 and row 3). In general, each pair of probes at row i can determine which column (north-south road) was used in coming from row i-1 and which column is taken to go to row i+1. That information is enough to determine the east-west directions on each row.

2. If you had only one probe, what is the minimum time it would take to guarantee to determine the outcome, assuming you could move the probe every hour?

You can guarantee to map out the tunnel in six hours. Test the points in Figure 1-25 in any order. Suppose every probe is negative in your first five attempts. No matter which probe point you leave out, there will be an ambiguity in the root (straight north up the center or a detour at the probe point still unexplored). You may be able to cut out early if a detour and a return to the central path has been detected, but this is not guaranteed.

3. If the tunnel is at most eight blocks long and begins at Start and ends at End, then what is the minimum number of point probe devices you would need to place to guarantee to determine the precise route of the tunnel in one hour?

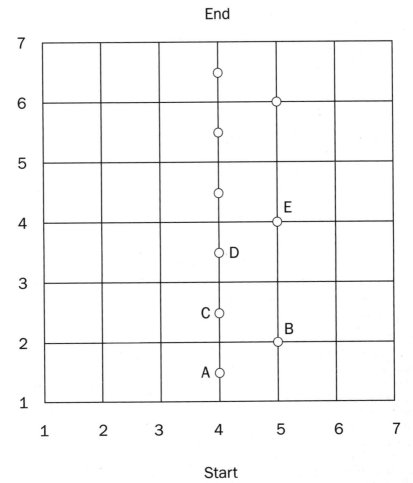

Figure 1-26: The center column's point probes tell whether the tunnel goes up the center line. If it misses the center, it must go either east or west. Because of the length limitation, it cannot go in both directions. Without reading the explanation, you may be able to figure out which column is taken between every pair of rows.

The problem can be solved with nine probes as in Figure 1-26.

From row 1 to row 2, the tunnel takes column 3 if neither probe A nor B detects it. The tunnel goes up column 4 if A detects it, and column 5 if B detects it but not A. From row 2 to row 3, the tunnel goes up column 3 if neither C nor B detects it, column 4 if C detects it, and column 5 if B is the only one that detects it. From row 3 to row 4, the story is similar. The tunnel takes column 3 if neither D nor E detects it, column 4 if D detects it and column 5 if E detects it. Row 4 is just like row 2, so the pattern continues.

4. **How few point probes could you use over two hours to guarantee to find the tunnel?**

In the first hour, just probe the center streets as in Figure 1-26. In the second hour, probe the eastern side of the first miss. If the tunnel is there, then it stays east until it rejoins the center. It cannot go to the western side because the tunnel is only eight blocks long.

Peter Carpenter of Wales contributed to these solutions. Tom Rokicki found the solutions for 3 and 4.

This problem becomes much more challenging if the tunnel could be longer. Solving it in general is an open problem.

Solution to Preferential Romance

1. **Are Bob and Alice compatible, passably compatible or neither? After dropping the smallest number of edges in zero, one, or both spouse's preferences, try to find a consistent ordering.**

They are passably compatible. Drop Bob's MC edge. (He should care more about culture, it seems.) Here is a consistent ordering: BRKCWFPOEMHTJ.

2. **Can you describe an algorithm for the counseling company to use to help marriages in distress? That is, try to find a method so spouses have to drop as few preferences as possible.**

The technique uses graph theory. Each circle in the figure is a "node" and each arrow represents a one-way edge. In graph-theoretic notation, let graph $G1 = (N1, E1)$, where $N1$ is a set of nodes and $E1$ is a set of directed (one-way) edges on those nodes. Similarly, $G2 = (N2, E2)$.

In the pseudo-code below, $\cup$ means set union. For example $\{X, Y, Z\} \cup \{Z, W\} = \{X, Y, Z, W\}$. Also, $\cap$ means set intersect. For example $\{X, Y, Z\} \cap \{Z, W\} = \{Z\}$. Finally, the minus sign (-) means set difference. For example $\{X, Y, Z\} - \{Z, W\} = \{X, Y\}$.

A cycle is a tour that starts at some node X and ends at X such that it always follows the one-way edges. A root is a node such that no one-way edge points to that node.

Here is the pseudo-code:

```
Given  G1 = (N1, E1) and G2 = (N2, E2)
H:= (N1 ∪ N2, E1 ∪ E2, EdgeMarks)
   where EdgeMarks is of the same size as E1 ∪ E2
   If e is in E1 ∩ E2, then e has a null mark.
   If e is in E1 - E2, then e has a mark of 1
   If e is in E2 - E1, then e has a mark of 2.
To find a consistent set of preferences, find the fewest
   edges having marks of 1 or 2 such that dropping them eliminates
   all cycles.
To find a consistent ordering, start at a root of H
   and write down its label. Then eliminate that root and
   edges leaving that root from H, then repeat.
```

This pseudo-code guarantees to find a consistent ordering, because any cycle-free graph will be consistent. To obtain a cycle-free graph, it is sufficient to eliminate marked edges, because unmarked ones are shared and we know that each spouse alone has produced a graph without cycles.

This is not quite an algorithm in that I did not tell you how to find the fewest edges to drop. In fact, that problem is NP-complete (a topic we'll discuss in Part II), so it is hard to find the fewest such edges, but heuristics such as simulated annealing (also discussed in Part II) work well.

Solution to No Change for the Holidays

1. **If you did not know how much the purchase price is except that it is a whole number amount between $1 and $100 inclusive, which amounts would you write on your three checks in order to minimize Claude's change?**

If the three checks are made out in the amounts of $15, $30, and $60, then you reduce the maximum change left with Claude to $14 no matter what the price. To see this, note that you can combine checks to sum up to $15, $30, $45, $60, $75, and $105. Because these sums differ by only $15, any amount between $1 and $100 is no more than $14 less than one of these sums.

2. **Suppose Claude publishes his four whole number prices in an advertisement that you see. Can you show how he can guarantee to do so in such a way that at least one item will yield him non-zero change no matter which three check amounts you write?**

Claude might publish $50, $51, $53, and $59. Suppose you try to find a set of checks that eliminates all change no matter which item your teenager selects. Some check must be $50 or less or the $50 item would require change. If $50, then another must be $1, so the third must be $8, because every item must be purchasable. In that case, the $53 would require change. If your teenager has no check for $50, but one for a lesser amount x, then your teenager also requires a check for $50 - $x. The remaining check must reach $59, so $51 and $53 will require change. Claude wins.

117

Solution to Quiet in the Depths

1. Assuming blood pressures are three digits long, can each department report one three digit number so that the captain can infer a blood pressure among the 10 middle blood pressures of the 25 sailors?

Each department sends back its median. Order them in ascending order and denote the medians as M1, M2, M3, M4, and M5 and their respective departmental groups as G1, G2, G3, G4, and G5. Figure 1-27 shows this ordering

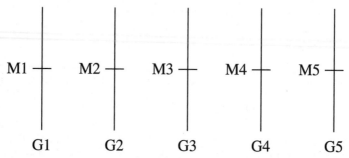

Figure 1-27: The groups have been ordered in ascending order based on their medians. Thus, M1 ≤ M2 ≤ M3 ≤ M4 ≤ M5. Within each group imagine low blood pressures to be at the bottom of the line segment corresponding to that group and high blood pressures near the top.

The number M3 must be one of the middle nine of the 25 blood pressure values. Here is why: Two sailors in G3 have blood pressures less than or equal to M3, the three lowest blood pressures of G2 must be less than or equal to M3, and the three lowest pressures of G1 must be less than or equal to M3. This means that at least 2 + 3 + 3 = 8 sailors must have lower or equal blood pressures to M3. Those are colored black in Figure 1-28.

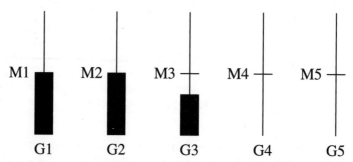

Figure 1-28: The dark rectangles represent values that are less than or equal to M3.

Symmetrically, at least eight sailors have blood pressures greater than or equal to M3. This means that M3 must be greater than or equal to at least eight values and less than or equal to at least eight values, so M3 is in the middle nine.

2. The captain wants to find some blood pressure value that is sure to be less than or equal to the median and some blood pressure value that is sure to be greater than or equal to the median. Using the assumptions of the first question, can the captain obtain such values after one three-digit report from each department?

Again the captain asks for the medians of each department. Ordering them again as M1, M2, M3, M4, and M5, the captain knows that M1 is less than or equal to the median of the 25 blood pressure values and M5 is greater than or equal to the median of the 25 values. Here is why: M1 is less than or equal to two blood pressure values of G1 and three from each of the groups G2, G3, G4, and G5 for a total of 14 values. These are shown in Figure 1-29. So M1 is certainly less than or equal to the median. Symmetrically, M5 is certainly greater than or equal to the median.

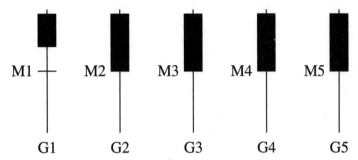

Figure 1-29: The dark rectangles represent values greater than or equal to M1.

Note: *The idea of using the median of the medians comes from "selection algorithms" for "order statistics." The paper that introduced this idea was written by some of the greatest algorithmists of all time: Blum, Floyd, Pratt, Rivest, and Tarjan.*

Part II

The Secret of the Puzzle

Ravi, Prasad, and I are working together still at the same software company. The founding partners of our company are always raving about how great it was to have recruited from the heuristics class.

—from a graduate of the Heuristic Problem Solving class at New York University

Part of the charm of puzzles is that they escape formulaic solutions. I often encounter students who do very well in calculus and discrete mathematics but find themselves stumped by puzzles whose reasoning requires only the most elementary algebra. Creativity is not the issue. Some people find the freedom offered by puzzles unfamiliar, and even slightly frightening. In this chapter, together, we will exorcise that fear demon.

The best puzzles may appear impossible at first, until you break them down, try alternatives, and finally solve them. The fact that a similar process is necessary in all large engineering and software projects is one reason that puzzles are used to screen job candidates. (A competing theory is that interviewers use puzzles to see people squirm. I'm not denying there is a little of that.)

If you had asked me a few years ago how to improve your puzzle-solving abilities, I would have recommended trying a lot of puzzles until you understood the patterns. But I've come to realize that certain patterns can be taught and their role in puzzles exposed. I've taught a class at New York University based on that belief, and it seems not only to hold, but also to be relevant to job success, as you can see from the quote that began this chapter. (By the way, I'm far from the first to create a course based on solving puzzles. Donald Knuth at Stanford and Ken Ross at Columbia had done similar courses before me, so I had existence proofs.)

Part II: The Secret of the Puzzle

Okay, I'm biased about the importance of puzzles. But my observation is that the problems people want to solve are often *NP-hard* (i.e., requiring an exhaustive search to guarantee to get the best answer—see the following sidebar). This is true whether you are doing register allocation in a compiler, or aligning genomes, or allocating seats on an airplane. You can, as a programmer, avoid such problems and write programs for accounts payable systems, but come on—the hard problems make our jobs fun.

What's an NP-hard Problem?

The term NP (non-deterministic polynomial) refers to the class of problems whose solutions can be verified in polynomial time in the size of the input. For example, if you ask me to find a route through 17 cities that will cost less than $3,000 and I present you a route R, you can easily compute the cost of route R by adding up 17 leg costs. In that case, the cost of verification would be linear in the number of cities, a polynomial of degree 1. Unfortunately, finding such a route may be much harder than verifying it. Intuitively, a problem is NP-complete if its solution can be **verified** in polynomial time, but there is no known polynomial time algorithm to **find** the solution. (A full formal definition would also go into the concept of reducibility, but we'll leave that to the textbooks.) For example, finding a route through a collection of cities that costs less than a certain amount is an NP-complete problem. By contrast, a problem is NP-hard if there is no known polynomial method to find an acceptable solution and possibly not even to verify one.

Since so many puzzles are *elimination* (or, if you wish, *constraint-oriented*) puzzles, we'll look at many of them in this chapter. The most familiar modern example of such a puzzle is Sudoku, though books of brainteasers are filled with other elimination puzzles. An elimination puzzle presents starting conditions, a set of constraints, and a target state. The goal is to reach the target state from the starting conditions while satisfying the constraints.

The reasoning these puzzles embody comes up often in design problems as well. At base, that reasoning entails a careful case analysis. Case analysis is fun if there are a small number of cases, but painful when there are many. For this reason, I present sample pseudocode in the examples here, and I encourage you to solve these puzzles in your favorite programming language.

Case analysis implies speculation, i.e., reasoning of the form: "Assume the following holds. Here are the consequences." Sometimes, the consequences are undesirable, so you must unroll one speculative guess and try another one. This kind of guess-and-test strategy works well for games as simple as Sudoku, because the number of speculations is well under 1,000 and usually more like 20.

When the number of guesses is large, you'll want to use other techniques. My standout favorite is dynamic programming. The classic example of dynamic programming is string edit distance (the basis for the diff program in Unix/Linux). Given two long strings, what is the shortest "edit sequence" of inserts, deletes, and single-letter rewrites that can convert one to the other? Go ahead and give it a try with these two invented genes: TGGAGACAGTCT and TAGATGGTCT.

Without dynamic programming, you could imagine lots of possible edit sequences, but it would be hard to know when you had found one of minimum cost. Dynamic programming offers a simple-to-program, efficient approach that is guaranteed to be optimal for this problem, as we'll see.

Unfortunately, dynamic programming doesn't solve all problems. NP-complete problems arise often and you will need to turn to heuristics to avoid an exhaustive search.[1] I'll give pseudo-code for my favorite heuristic technique — simulated annealing — and will invite you to try it out on some NP-hard puzzles. We'll start easy. If you have trouble along the way, note that the solutions to early puzzles offer techniques you can use for the later ones.

---

[1]Russians prefer the term "perebor," which means brute force, to exhaustive search— I like the feeling of that term. I imagine a hardy Russian bear doing perebor on a beehive.

THE PUZZLES

Order the Ages

Urban Planning

Finding a Schedule that Works

Picturing the Treasure

Sudoku

Number Encoding

Selective Greed

Sweet Packs

Revisiting a Traveling Salesman

Overloaded Scheduling and Freezing Crystals

Wordsnakes

Maximal Friends

Winning at the Slots

Understanding Dice

Bait and Switch

Order the Ages

You might encounter elimination puzzles like this one in Mensa-style books. As mental calisthenics, they have a lot to recommend them.

Andrew, Carol, Jessica, Luke, and Tommy are sitting around a circular table. Carol is 12 years older than her neighbor to the left. Tommy is five years older than his neighbor to the right. Jessica is 14 years older than her neighbor to the left. Luke is five years younger than his neighbor to the left. By age, from youngest to oldest, they are ordered as follows: Luke, Tommy, Andrew, Jessica, and Carol. Luke is 16 and Carol is 40. The total of the ages is 135. In which order are the people sitting (starting with Tommy and then proceeding in clockwise order) and what are their ages? First try to do this on your own; when you've solved it or are ready for help, read on.

Start with the most specific facts: Luke is 16 and Carol is 40, totaling 56. This implies that the ages of Tommy, Andrew, and Jessica add up to 79 (135 - 56 = 79). Further, we know that Tommy and Luke are neighbors because Luke's left neighbor is 21, so if that's not Tommy, then both Tommy and Luke's left neighbors are 21 or less (because Tommy is second youngest after Luke). This leaves 79 - 42 = 37 left for the last person. But Carol is 12 years older than her neighbor to the left, so someone must be 28 years old. Hence, in clockwise order we must have Tommy, then Luke. This means that Tommy, Luke, and Carol total 21 + 16 + 40 = 77.

Therefore, Jessica and Andrew total 135 - 77 = 58. Because Jessica is known to be older than Andrew and the person to the left of Carol must be 28 years old, Andrew is 28 and Jessica is 30.

The ages then lend insight to the seating. Ordering Tommy, Luke, and then Carol is impossible because Carol is 40. This implies that Carol's left neighbor is Andrew, since we know he is 28.

This leaves two possibilities:

Tommy, Luke, Jessica, Andrew, Carol

Tommy, Luke, Andrew, Carol, Jessica

But in fact only the first one is possible because Jessica is 14 years older than her neighbor to the left. That can only be Luke. So we conclude:

Tommy(21), Luke (16), Jessica (30), Andrew (28), Carol(40)

What would you do if you wanted to solve many puzzles like this in a short time? When the numbers are this small, I suggest laying out all orders and then filling in numbers starting with the ones you know to see if they work. In this case, once you arrived at the correct ordering, you would have started with

Tommy, Luke (16), Jessica, Andrew, Carol (40)

and then filled in the other numbers based on constraints:

Tommy (21), Luke (16), Jessica (30), Andrew (28), Carol (40)

When the number of orders is too large, this can't be done, of course. In that case, you would need to determine local orderings (as we did for Tommy and Luke) and then order the rest.

The point, however, is that the following simple algorithm works really nicely for many puzzles:

```
for each ordering R
  try to verify constraints
  reject R if some constraint fails
end for
```

Replacing difficult analysis by a program that tries lots of possibilities without much human tinkering is a recurrent theme in this chapter. Purists may object that having the computer race through many choices mindlessly is a travesty of thought. My first reaction: So be it. My second: Thought will return soon enough in the form of a better algorithmic approach when the number of cases explodes.

Urban Planning

Constraint problems arise in many settings. Urban planning presents a particularly attractive challenge because it mixes geometry with logic. Your job in this puzzle is to lay out a town into city blocks under certain constraints.

In what follows, distance is measured in Manhattan distance: The distance between blocks A and B is the number of east-west streets plus the number of north-south streets between their nearest corners. Thus, if block B lies immediately due east of block A, the distance between them is 1. If B lies southwest of A and traveling from the northeast corner of block B to the southwest corner of block A requires crossing five east-west streets and two north-south streets, then the distance between the two blocks is seven.

Here are the constraints. The industrial zone (I) and every housing complex (H) should be at least eight blocks apart. Each office building (O) and each housing complex (H) should be between two and six blocks apart, inclusive. Every housing complex (H) should be within two blocks of some shopping center (S). Every shopping center (S) should be within one block of a warehouse (W). Each warehouse (W) should be within six blocks of the industrial zone (I). Each housing complex (H) should be within one block of a park (P). Unused lots can be laid out as vacant (X).

Each block contains only one activity. There are five blocks of housing complexes, two of shopping centers, one industrial, two warehouses, and three office buildings. You will decide on the number of parks you need.

1. If the town is to be laid out as a square, how many blocks on each side must the town have as a minimum?

2. Given the size determined from your answer to the first question, find a layout that leaves the largest possible (in area) rectangle of vacant blocks (X) or parkland (P). Your customers are thinking of building a stadium there. Show the layout.

3. If one constraint were eliminated, how many blocks on each side would this town need to be at a minimum, disregarding the stadium? Say which constraint should be eliminated and show the layout.

Solution to Urban Planning

1. If the town is to be laid out as a square, how many blocks on each side must the town have as a minimum?

It has to be at least six by six, because of the minimum distance constraint between industrials and housing. Under that constraint, even five by five would be unacceptable for more than one housing unit. The constraint also implies that the industrial zone must be in one corner.

2. Given the size determined from your answer to the first question, find a layout that leaves the largest possible (in area) rectangle of vacant blocks (X) or parkland (P). Your customers are thinking of building a stadium there. Show the layout.

Figure 2-1 shows a possible layout. The stadium could be 3 by 5, hence *could have* an area of 15.

I	X	X	X	X	X
X	X	X	O	O	O
X	X	X	X	W	S
X	X	X	W	P	H
X	X	X	S	H	H
X	X	P	H	H	P

Figure 2-1: I is an industrial block, O is an office block, W is a warehouse block, S a shopping block, H a housing block, P a park, and X vacant. The industrial zone must be far from the housing.

3. If one constraint were eliminated, how many blocks on each side would this town need to be at a minimum, disregarding the stadium? Say which constraint should be eliminated and show the layout.

If you eliminate the constraint separating industrial zones from housing, say by finding non-polluting industrials, then the town could fit into the lower right 4 by 4 square, shown in Figure 2-2. There could be a large belt of vacant land.

X	X	X	X	X	X
X	X	X	X	X	X
X	X	I	O	W	S
X	X	O	W	P	H
X	X	O	S	H	H
X	X	P	H	H	P

Figure 2-2: Because the industry is clean, the industrial zone can be folded among the other uses, yielding a 4 by 4 square.

Finding a Schedule That Works

You have a set of tasks for a robot. There is no precedence constraint requiring any task to be completed before another. Each requires a certain amount of time and has a certain deadline. Your predecessor assures you there is enough time for the robot to do everything, but he doesn't remember how. (His lack of organization explains why he is your predecessor and not your boss.) You have to arrange things so your robot finishes each task by its deadline.

1. In which order do you schedule the tasks starting from current day 0?

Task T1 takes 4 days with deadline on day 45

Task T2 takes 4 days with deadline on day 48

Task T3 takes 5 days with deadline on day 25

Task T4 takes 2 days with deadline on day 49

Task T5 takes 5 days with deadline on day 36

Task T6 takes 2 days with deadline on day 31

Task T7 takes 7 days with deadline on day 9

Task T8 takes 5 days with deadline on day 39

Task T9 takes 4 days with deadline on day 13

Task T10 takes 6 days with deadline on day 17

Task T11 takes 4 days with deadline on day 29

Task T12 takes 1 day with deadline on day 19

Hint: The best algorithm for this problem has the very suggestive name: "Earliest Deadline First."

Solution to Finding a Schedule That Works

1. In which order do you schedule the tasks starting from current day 0?

This is a situation where you don't want the computer to explore all cases, trying all 12! Orderings might take a while and would be completely impractical if there were even 20 tasks. As alluded to in the hint, there is an efficient scheduling algorithm with a very suggestive name: Earliest Deadline First. In fact, the name is the algorithm. That is, you first do the task with the earliest deadline and continue to do every other task in deadline order. In this case, the algorithm gives us an ordering:

```
T7 T9 T10 T12 T3 T11 T6 T5 T8 T1 T2 T4
```

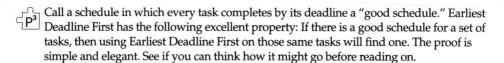 Call a schedule in which every task completes by its deadline a "good schedule." Earliest Deadline First has the following excellent property: If there is a good schedule for a set of tasks, then using Earliest Deadline First on those same tasks will find one. The proof is simple and elegant. See if you can think how it might go before reading on.

Suppose that in a good schedule S, task T executes just before T′ even though T has a later deadline than T′. Suppose further that T is the first task for which this is true. Because both T and T′ complete before their deadlines, swapping the two will still enable them to complete before their deadlines. (To be concrete, suppose that T has deadline d and T′ has deadline d′. By assumption d′ < d. In the original schedule, both T and T′ complete by their deadlines, so both finish by time d′. Swapping them will preserve that property.) Thus, we can always transform a good schedule into another one in which tasks execute in deadline order.

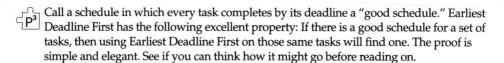 Unfortunately, sometimes a system is overloaded, and that can change Earliest Deadline First from a great strategy to a really poor one. For example, what is the shortest task you could add to the above list to cause Earliest Deadline First to miss every deadline? For now, assume that your robot will continue working on a task T even after its deadline has passed, provided T has the earliest deadline of all uncompleted tasks. Give it a try.

A task requiring 3 days with deadline 2 or earlier will do it. That new task will fail to complete by its deadline and will cause every other task to miss its deadline as well.

Working on a task after its deadline has passed may seem foolish. It would be far better to drop some tasks and complete others. We'll work on such a strategy in the puzzle "Overloaded Scheduling and Freezing Crystals." The fundamental point here is that a naive greedy approach can be brittle, that is, it may work well until a certain load and then cease to work entirely.

Picturing the Treasure

The previous three puzzles all had a generic, though inefficient, solution strategy: Try all possible rearrangements and see if any meet the constraints. This one demands geometrical insight.

A pirate's trunk filled with millions of dollars worth of jewels is buried in the sand on a flat part of the deep ocean floor. Your client has dropped sensors in the area to try to locate the trunk. The sensors can be dropped to a precise location, but their reports of distance to the treasure trunk are accurate only to within 10 percent. The first sensor reports the treasure to be at a distance of 450 meters (so the real distance from that sensor falls between 405 meters and 495 meters). A second sensor reports the treasure to be at 350 meters (real distance is between 315 meters and 385 meters). Because your client doesn't want you to hire your own ship, he tells you only relative positions of the sensors. Specifically, he tells you the first sensor is at position (0,0) and the second is at position (300, 400).

Warm-Up

 If the sensor estimates of distance to the treasure were precisely correct (no plus or minus 10 percent), how could you use one more sensor to find the exact position of the treasure?

Solution to Warm-Up

Draw a circle of radius 450 around (0,0) and another circle of radius 350 around (300, 400). The two circles meet at two points, as you can see in Figure 2-3.

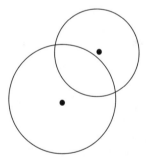

Figure 2-3: The larger circle has a radius of 450 meters and the smaller has a radius of 350 meters. Their centers at (0,0) and (300,400) are 500 meters apart by the Pythagorean theorem.

Finding these two points algebraically is a bit of a challenge. Start with the two equations for the circles:

(1) $x^2 + y^2 = 450^2 = 202{,}500$

(2) $(x-300)^2 + (y-400)^2 = 350^2 = 122{,}500$

Part II: The Secret of the Puzzle

After suitable subtractions, you get the following equation for the line containing the chord linking the intersection points:

$$3x + 4y = 1{,}650$$

Substituting for the y value into equation (1) yields:

$$x^2 + (-3x/4 + 412.5)^2 = x^2 + 9x^2/16 - 618.75x + 170{,}156.2 = 202{,}500$$

Solving the quadratic and substituting back into the equation for the chord line gives two intersection points:

$$(-46.75,\ 447.56) \text{ and } (442.75,\ 80.44)$$

The geometrical approach (even a scribbled picture) is vastly better and leads immediately to the instruction: Place a sensor on one of these intersection points. Either the sensor lands on the treasure or the treasure is at the other intersection point. In fact, you could place a sensor anywhere closer to one intersection point than the other.

Unfortunately, the distance between the sensors and the treasure is accurate only to within 10 percent, as noted. Please answer the questions in that imperfect world:

1. Where would you place a third sensor to guarantee the most accurate estimate possible of the location of the treasure trunk?

2. Suppose your client gave you two more sensors (that is, a third and fourth) that have to be dropped simultaneously. Could you find the treasure to within a single rectangle whose area is well under 5,000 square meters? How about under 2,000 square meters?

3. Suppose you had been called in before the first two sensors were dropped, but you were given only three sensors altogether. Two were extremely accurate (to within a centimeter) whereas the other was accurate only to within 10%. Assuming you had to drop two sensors at positions (0,0) and (300,400), in which order should you drop the sensors and which sensors should you use when and where to be able to locate the treasure to the smallest possible rectangular area?

Solution to Picturing the Treasure

1. Where would you place a third sensor to guarantee the most accurate estimate possible of the location of the treasure trunk?

Augment each circle with an inner circle and an outer circle corresponding to the possible distances, as shown in Figure 2-4.

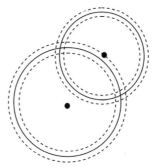

Figure 2-4: The larger circle has a bigger uncertainty, reflecting the 10% accuracy.

Once again, if you put a sensor at one of the nominal intersection points (say the same one you would have used in the warm-up), either you will find that the treasure is within 60 meters or that it is hundreds of meters away. In that case, it is within 60 meters of the other nominal intersection point. Why 60 meters? Because $60 > \sqrt{((35^2) + (45^2))}$ and the rectangles are approximately 70 by 90. However, one can step literally "out of the box" and get a better solution, as suggested by Ivan Rezanka. If we placed the third sensor along the line segment between center points (-46.75, 447.56) and (442.75, 80.44) but, say, closer to (-46.75, 447.56), then we could distinguish which rectangle the treasure is in and obtain even a more accurate estimate within that rectangle. The best place to put that sensor is a problem I leave to you.

2. Suppose your client gave you two more sensors (that is, a third and fourth) that have to be dropped simultaneously. Could you find the treasure to within a single rectangle whose area is well under 5,000 square meters? How about under 2,000 square meters?

As mentioned, the first two sensors limit the search to two rectangles of lengths 70 meters by 90 meters. These are centered at the points of exact intersection: (-46.75, 447.56) and (442.75, 80.44). You might think it could be a good idea to put the two sensors in the centers of the two rectangles. However, if we consider the case of each rectangle, then we realize that we might be better off to put the sensor in the right rectangle. For example, suppose we put each sensor 30 meters from the center along the center line and parallel to the longer side of the rectangle (see Figure 2-5).

If the sensor is within 38.1 meters of the treasure, then the treasure is limited to the right half of the rectangle plus less than half of the left half of the rectangle, a total rectangular area of less than 53.1 by 70, as illustrated in Figure 2-6. (Why 38.1? Because 38.1 is the distance between the right upper and lower corners of the rectangle and the sensor position.)

Because of the 10% inaccuracy, however, the sensor might be within 38.1 meters of the treasure, yet the device would read 42.3 meters (that is, 4.2 meters more). Moreover, such a reading could also be approximately 4.2 meters too little. This limits the accuracy to (15 + 42.3 + 4.2) by 70, which is under 4,310 square meters. If the sensor reading is greater than 42.3 meters of the treasure, we would know for sure that the treasure is limited to those portions of the rectangle not completely covered by the circle (70 by 60).

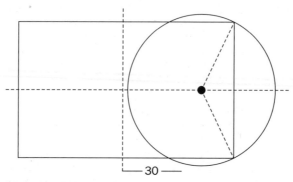

Figure 2-5: For each approximate rectangle surrounding an intersection point, put the sensor 30 meters to the right of the center of the rectangle. Thus, not only will one know which rectangle contains the treasure, but also more or less where in the rectangle. For example, if the sensor reading is greater than 42.3 meters, then the treasure trunk is in the subrectangle to the right of the portion completely covered by the circle.

However, that second number is conservative. For example, if the measured distance is 50, then the rectangle encompassing the treasure ranges from roughly 28 to the left of the sensor to 55 away from the sensor in the horizontal direction, describing a rectangle of sides (55 - 28) by 70 having an area of 1,890 square meters.

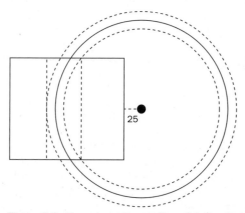

Figure 2-6: Given a sensor reading of d, the sketch shows the nominal circle, the smaller error circle (dashed), and the larger error circle (dashed). The treasure must be inside the dotted rectangle.

This leads to a much better approach (see Figure 2-6). Consider placing the sensor 25 meters to the right of the right border of each 70 by 90 rectangle (that is, 70 meters from the center of the rectangle), assuming the 90 meter long borders of the rectangle are horizontal. Any distance from the sensor would describe an arc through the rectangle. If that distance were d, then the leftmost point within the rectangle would be d - 25 to the left of the right border of the rectangle (and would lie on the center line of the rectangle). The rightmost points would be where the arc intersects the top and bottom edges of the rectangle, as you can see in the figure. There would be two rightmost points at the upper and lower rectangular edges. Their position can be determined by the Pythagorean theorem. Since a sensor reading of d could mean an actual distance between 0.9d and 1.1d, we will take the leftmost point from the 1.1d reading and the rightmost point from the 0.9d reading. So, choosing this position for the sensor gives us a single rectangle to search whose area is under 1,940 square meters.

3. **Suppose you had been called in before the first two sensors were dropped, but you were given only three sensors. Two were extremely accurate (to within a centimeter), whereas the other was accurate only to within 10%. Assuming you had to drop two sensors at positions (0,0) and (300,400), in which order should you drop the sensors and which sensors should you use when and where to be able to locate the treasure to the smallest possible rectangular area?**

This question turns out to be surprisingly easy to answer. Use the accurate sensors at positions (0,0) and (300,400). By the argument in the warm-up, that leaves only two tiny areas where the treasure could be. The inaccurate sensor could be used to decide which area had the sensor. What's counterintuitive is that one might think it better to use the inaccurate sensor first and then use the accurate ones. A follow-up question is what to do if you have three sensors, all of different accuracies.

Sudoku

I was introduced to Sudoku when my 12-year-old asked me to solve the most challenging one in a book while on a train. Because attempting a solution on a moving train made me slightly sick, I resolved to solve the game by programming. Three hours and 100 lines of programming later, my program could solve the hardest Sudoku puzzles I found on the Web in two seconds. I'm not boasting. The current brevity record for a Sudoku-solving program that I know of is by Arthur Whitney in his programming language q. It's 103 *characters* long. Now, I do not advocate short program contests, because I think they lead to incomprehensible code, but I do find this impressive.

Let's study Sudoku as an elimination puzzle. The target state is to fill a 9 by 9 grid with digits between 1 and 9. Each digit should appear exactly once in each row, once in each column, and once in each non-overlapping three by three box starting from the upper left corner.

Warm-Up

Consider the following Sudoku puzzle:

								7
7		4				8	9	3
		6	8		2			
		7	5	2	8	6		
	8				6	7		1
9		3	4				8	
			7		4	9		
6				9				
4	5	9				1		8

Below, we use 0 to represent a blank square.

0	0	0	0	0	0	0	0	7
7	0	4	0	0	0	8	9	3
0	0	6	8	0	2	0	0	0
0	0	7	5	2	8	6	0	0
0	8	0	0	0	6	7	0	1
9	0	3	4	0	0	0	8	0
0	0	0	7	0	4	9	0	0
6	0	0	0	9	0	0	0	0
4	5	9	0	0	0	1	0	8

Let's look at the lower left box in context:

0	0	0						
7	0	4						
0	0	6						
0	0	7						
0	8	0						
9	0	3						
0	0	0	7	0	4	9	0	0
6	0	0	0	9	0	0	0	0
4	5	9	0	0	0	1	0	8

We know that of the five zeroes present in the lower left box, one must be 7 and one must be 8. Because there is a 7 on the row that is third from bottom, none of the top zeroes can be changed to a 7. Because there is a 7 in the third column, the only place for a 7 is to the right of the 6, yielding:

0	0	0						
7	0	4						
0	0	6						
0	0	7						
0	8	0						
9	0	3						
0	0	0	7	0	4	9	0	0
6	7	0	0	9	0	0	0	0
4	5	9	0	0	0	1	0	8

Part II: The Secret of the Puzzle

This now implies, in the right lower box, that the 7 must be on the last row, yielding this:

0	0	0						
7	0	4						
0	0	6						
0	0	7						
0	8	0						
9	0	3						
0	0	0	7	0	4	9	0	0
6	7	0	0	9	0	0	0	0
4	5	9	0	0	0	1	7	8

Working an example by hand often suggests an algorithm. That is the case here. Start by annotating each 0 by the values it could have. Those are the constraints on that position. Whenever a 0 can have only one value, replace it by that value and recompute the constraints on all other 0s.

Let's do this starting from the puzzle as it now stands:

0	0	0	0	0	0	0	0	7
7	0	4	0	0	0	8	9	3
0	0	6	8	0	2	0	0	0
0	0	7	5	2	8	6	0	0
0	8	0	0	0	6	7	0	1
9	0	3	4	0	0	0	8	0
0	0	0	7	0	4	9	0	0
6	7	0	0	9	0	0	0	0
4	5	9	0	0	0	1	7	8

Start with the top left corner 0 and give its context:

0	0	0	0	0	0	0	0	7
7	0	4						
0	0	6						
0								
0								
9								
0								
6								
4								

That entry can be any number between 1 and 9, provided it is not 4, 6, 7, or 9. That is, it could be 1, 2, 3, 5, or 8. This is not very constraining. Let us next consider the middle entry of the upper left box:

0	0	0						
7	0	4	0	0	0	8	9	3
0	0	6						
	0							
	8							
	0							
	0							
	7							
	5							

It cannot be 3, 4, 5, 6, 7, 8, 9. So, it is limited to 1 or 2. That is better, but not great yet.

Continue testing the possibilities for each 0 to see if you can find one that has only one possible value. For example, consider the top left entry of the middle left box:

0								
7								
0								
0	0	7	5	2	8	6	0	0
0	8	0						
9	0	3						
0								
6								
4								

The following are excluded: 2, 3, 4, 5, 6, 7, 8, 9. So this value must be 1, yielding a new state:

0	0	0	0	0	0	0	0	7
7	0	4	0	0	0	8	9	3
0	0	6	8	0	2	0	0	0
1	0	7	5	2	8	6	0	0
0	8	0	0	0	6	7	0	1
9	0	3	4	0	0	0	8	0
0	0	0	7	0	4	9	0	0
6	7	0	0	9	0	0	0	0
4	5	9	0	0	0	1	7	8

Now, let's look just to the right of that entry. Here is the context:

	0							
	0							
	0							
1	0	7	5	2	8	6	0	0
0	8	0						
9	0	3						
	0							
	7							
	5							

This excludes 1, 2, 3, 5, 6, 7, 8, 9. So this forces a choice of 4. (We can use more context sometimes, such as the fact that the first column has a 4, thus precluding a 4 from replacing the 0 between the 1 and the 9, but don't try such reasoning in a moving train.) Go ahead. Try to solve this one. You'll see that it's pretty easy.

Solution to Warm-Up

8	1	5	3	4	9	2	6	7
7	2	4	6	5	1	8	9	3
3	9	6	8	7	2	4	1	5
1	4	7	5	2	8	6	3	9
5	8	2	9	3	6	7	4	1
9	6	3	4	1	7	5	8	2
2	3	1	7	8	4	9	5	6
6	7	8	1	9	5	3	2	4
4	5	9	2	6	3	1	7	8

In the warm-up puzzle, there was always at least one entry that was constrained to a single value. That is, we were never tempted to "speculate" — assign a value to an entry that is consistent with the constraints, but is not the only possibility, and then explore the implications. Let's see if we can design an algorithm.

Here is the pseudo-code without speculation (basicsud):

```
proc basicsud(state s)
  stillchanging:= true
  while stillchanging
   stillchanging:= false
   find constraints for each entry currently represented by a 0 in s
   if there is only one possible value v for some entry e then
         assign v to e in s
         stillchanging:= true
   end if
   if there is an entry e with no possible values then
         return "inconsistent state"
   end if
  end while
  return s
end proc
```

Part II: The Secret of the Puzzle

This routine works not only for easy Sudokus, but it is also the workhorse for the harder ones. Hard Sudokus require speculation and therefore the test for the inconsistent case when the speculation doesn't work out. An inconsistency might arise, for example, when the row and the column of an entry together already include all numbers between 1 and 9.

How does speculation work? Let's start with the intuition. Assume that we have a consistent state to begin with. We call basicsud. If this leads to a complete state (one with every blank/zero entry replaced by a number), then we are done. If we reach a point where every blank entry has two or more possible values, we systematically try the possible values for each entry. That is, for each current blank, we will save the current state, and then try one of its values. If that attempt (or speculation) leads to an inconsistent state, then restore the state before the speculation and try another value.

The pseudo-code (specsud) makes use of a stack in which we save states as we go. When we're about to speculate, we push a state onto the stack. If the speculation doesn't work, we pop the top state from the stack.

```
proc specsud(state s)
    s':= basicsud(s)
    if s' == "inconsistent state" then
         return "inconsistent state"
    end if
    if s' is complete then return s'
     else
       let R be the entries in s'
            having two or more possible values
       for each entry e in R
         let V be the possible values for e
         for each value v in V
            push s' on the stack of saved states
            s'':= s' with the assignment of v to e
            s''':=  specsud(s'')
            if s''' is complete then return s''' end if
            pop s'
         end for
       end for
    end if
end proc specsud
```

This algorithm is easy to program in almost every language and the resulting code runs in less than a second. See if you can solve the following problem in three seconds or less on a late-model personal computer. The 103-character program I referred to above takes under 100 milliseconds, but this is not a race. Really. It's not.

1. Find the solution to this Sudoku.

0	3	0	0	0	0	0	4	0
0	1	0	0	9	7	0	5	0
0	0	2	5	0	8	6	0	0
0	0	3	0	0	0	8	0	0
9	0	0	0	0	4	3	0	0
0	0	7	6	0	0	0	0	4
0	0	9	8	0	5	4	0	0
0	7	0	0	0	0	0	2	0
0	5	0	0	7	1	0	8	0

Solution to Sudoku

1. **Find the solution to this Sudoku.**

Here is the solution to the challenging Sudoku. I simply programmed the solver I outlined in pseudo-code. There are remarkably few backtracks — under 50.

8	3	5	1	2	6	7	4	9
4	1	6	3	9	7	2	5	8
7	9	2	5	4	8	6	3	1
6	4	3	9	1	2	8	7	5
9	8	1	7	5	4	3	6	2
5	2	7	6	8	3	1	9	4
2	6	9	8	3	5	4	1	7
1	7	8	4	6	9	5	2	3
3	5	4	2	7	1	9	8	6

Incidentally, the following Sudoku variant may exist, but I haven't found it yet. I call it *Sudokill*. It is a two-person game. Let's say I'm playing against you. We alternate laying numbers down on a Sudoku board. I win if I leave you no number to lay down, either because the board is complete or because any number you put down is inconsistent with the constraints. Similarly, you win if you can prevent me from moving.

Number Encoding

The idea of speculating given a set of constraints is such a common notion that you might want to try it again in a different setting.

In this puzzle, you are given several groups of 2 to 9 letters. Each group encodes an ascending consecutive run of numbers, e.g. 2, 3, 4, 5. In the simplest version of this puzzle, each letter encodes a single number between 1 and 9. Your job is to find the encoding.

Warm-Up

Assume this simplest encoding. Find the single number represented by each letter. Suppose the groups you see are:

```
GDF
IHEC
DFBIH
FBIHECA
HE
FBIH
IHE
FBIHEC
BIHE
EC
FB
```

Solution to Warm-Up

Because each group represents an ascending run of numbers, FBIHEC represents a subsequence of the numbers of FBIHECA, so it doesn't tell anything new. In general, we don't care about any groups that are subsequences of others. This leaves us with GDF, DFBIH, and FBIHECA. Putting the first and third of these together, you get GDFBIHECA. So, G = 1, D = 2, ..., A = 9.

That was just a warm-up. Now consider the case where a letter can represent two numbers.

Part II: The Secret of the Puzzle

1. Can you figure out which (up to) two numbers each letter represents?

EDHFHI	FDBFHI
ACBEDHG	BFEBGDI
HFD	IEDH
EEBGH	EHG
HGH	FEBGH
FEBF	CBEEBF
IEDBFDG	CIFD
ACBFEB	EEB
CBEEHGDG	ED
ACIFEHG	FEBG
CIFE	CIEEH
BFDH	

2. For those who are gluttons for punishment, what are the up to three encodings for each letter given this list of groups?

ABBDH	DCHGEBF
AFCFAE	ADCFAEG
EBFG	IAAGIB
ADCI	HBBDB
IHBID	FCFGAII
DCIHEI	FCHGBG
AFCFA	EIDG
DCFGAB	ABBDB
FCIH	GEI
HAE	AI
CFGAGF	DCIAE
EIDB	BIIB
AEB	BIDH
EBD	AABF
EGD	EDCIHE
CIHBBI	CFABB
AIF	GDB
HBID	GIH
EFCI	HGAG
HABG	FCI
BIFG	DCHGBBDH
FCHABI	FGEGF
ABID	BIFH
CFHEB	

Solution to Number Encoding

1. **Can you figure out which (up to) two numbers each letter represents?**

Here is the solution for the case in which a single letter may represent up to two letters.

A is 1; B is 3 or 6; C is 2; D is 5 or 8; E is 4 or 5; F is 4 or 7; G is 7 or 9; H is 6 or 8; I is 3 or 9.

2. **For those who are gluttons for punishment, what are the up to three encodings for each letter given this list of groups?**

Here is a solution in the case when each single letter can represent up to three letters.

A is 1, 5, or 6; B is 6, 7, or 9; C is 3; D is 2 or 8; E is 1 or 6; F is 2, 4, or 8; G is 5, 7, or 9; H is 4, 5 or 9; I is 4, 7, or 8.

Selective Greed

So far, except for our preview of overloaded scheduling and our use of speculation, the best strategy has smacked of a "follow your nose" (also known as *greedy*) approach:

If a move lowers the cost/gets closer to the solution, take it; otherwise, avoid it.

Sometimes that basic philosophy works but requires a slight modification:

Find the lowest cost solutions to subproblems, and then glue the solutions to the best subproblems together.

Welcome to dynamic programming. This is a technique with an enormous number of applications. We'll start with string editing, but soon you'll be planning menus.

The string edit problem is to convert a source string to a target string in the fewest number of "edits" possible. There are three kinds of edits: changing a letter (e.g., 'a' becomes 'b'), inserting a letter (e.g., replace a blank by 'c'), and deleting a letter (e.g., replacing 'c' by a blank). For example, to edit the word 'rent' to the semantically equivalent (if you live in the United Kingdom) 'let', we would change 'r' to 'l' and delete 'n'. To go the other way, we would change 'l' to 'r' and insert 'n'. The other letters don't change. Either way, the *edit distance* is 2.

Warm-Up

When the words are short, it is easy to find an answer by eye, but consider this example inspired by genomics.

How many edits are needed to convert 'TAGATGGTCT' to 'TGGAGACAGTCT'? Go ahead and give it a try.

Solution to Warm-Up

To understand the dynamic programming approach to this problem, consider a small conversion example: 'AGA' to 'TGGAG'. For the moment, resist the temptation to do this by eye and take a look at the matrix in Figure 2-7.

		T	G	G	A	G
	0	1	2	3	4	5
A	1					
G	2					
A	3					

Figure 2-7: The beginning of the dynamic programming matrix. The top row represents the number of inserts to go from an empty string to, respectively, an empty string, a string consisting of 'T' alone, a string consisting of 'TG', and so on. The left column represents the number of deletes to go to an empty string from, respectively, an empty string, a string consisting of 'A', a string consisting of 'AG', and a string consisting of 'AGA'.

We've written 'TGGAG' above the matrix and 'AGA' to the left of the matrix. The number in the top row of the matrix corresponds to the number of inserts, in turn, required to go from the empty string to the empty string (0), from the empty string to 'T' (1), from the empty string to 'TG' (2), and so on up to 5. The leftmost column corresponds to the number of deletes to go, in turn, from the empty string to the empty string (0), from 'A' to the empty string (1), and so on. That ends the setup phase.

Now we will fill in the matrix row by row. Location $(0, 0)$, that is row 0, column 0, is the top left corner. Row i, column j will correspond to the edit distance between letters 1 through i of 'AGA' and 1 through j of 'TGGAG'. As we fill in the entry for row i, column j, we will already have filled in entries for row i-1, column j (the entry above), row i, column j-1 (the entry to the left), and row i-1, column j-1 (the entry that is the upper left diagonal). We will use those values as well as the ith letter of 'AGA' and the jth letter of 'TGGAG' to determine the entry for row i, column j.

In the following formula, `differs(i,j)` will be 1 if the ith letter of 'AGA' differs from the jth letter of 'TGGAG' and 0 otherwise.

```
entry(row i, column j) = min(entry(row i-1, column j) + 1,
  entry(row i, column j-1) + 1,
  entry(row i-1, column j-1) + differs(i,j))
```

Look at the entry under the T and in the row of the first A in Figure 2-8.

151

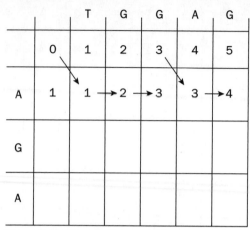

Figure 2-8: Filling in the second row corresponds to the problem of transforming 'A' to 'TGGAG'. As you can see from the arrows, the best thing to do is to insert 'TGG' and then 'G' along with a zero-cost replacement of 'A' by 'A'.

The arrow indicates that the value in that square comes from the upper left diagonal neighbor, because 0 + differs(1,1) = 0 + 1 = 1 is less than what could have been obtained from coming from the left (1 + 1 = 2) or from above (1 + 1 = 2). So, in this case, the cheapest way to edit from 'A' to 'T' is to replace 'A' by 'T'. The alternative coming from the left would be: Delete 'A' and then insert 'T' for a cost of 2. The alternative from the top would be: Insert 'T' and then delete 'A'. The entry under the first G could come either from its upper left diagonal neighbor or from the left. The way we've drawn it, the path until this point says "to go from A to TG, replace A by T and insert G." This corresponds to an edit distance of 2.

Now go two to the right (to the entry under the A). In this case, the cheapest path is from the upper left diagonal which has a value 3. Note that differ(1,4) = 0, because the first character of 'AGA' and the fourth character of 'TGGAG' are both 'A'. This corresponds to inserting 'T', 'G', 'G' (at a cost of 3) and then replacing 'A' by 'A' (at a cost of 0). The last entry is at a cost of 4, because it corresponds to the above steps followed by the insertion of 'G'. The point is that each square is filled in by looking at just its three neighbors: left, up, and upper left.

Now we are ready for the next row. In Figure 2-9, notice that the entry to the right of the G in 'AGA' and beneath the first G in 'TGGAG' is 1 and it is less than its neighbors to the left and above. That entry corresponds to replacing 'A' by 'T' and 'G' by 'G'. The rightmost entry of that G row corresponds to inserting 'T', 'G', and 'G', and then replacing the 'A' by 'A' and the 'G' by 'G'.

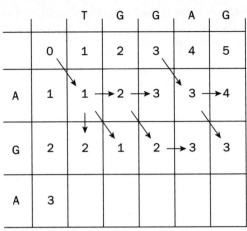

Figure 2-9: Filling in the third row of the dynamic programming matrix plus indications of some possible best paths, though not all of them.

By now, you should understand the idea well enough to be able to trace the path for the full solution, as shown in Figure 2-10.

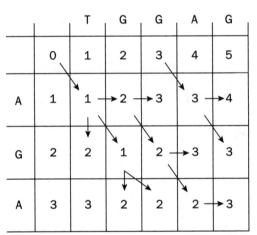

Figure 2-10: The entire matrix for the warm-up. In the end, we match 'GA' with 'GA' and insert or relabel for the rest.

The path to the lower right corresponds to replace 'A' by 'T', insert 'G', replace 'G' by 'G', replace 'A' by 'A' and insert 'G'. This gives an optimal cost of 3. There is one other optimal editing pattern: Replace 'A' by 'T', replace 'G' by 'G', insert 'G', replace 'A' by 'A', and insert 'G'.

Part II: The Secret of the Puzzle

Dynamic programming is a greedy method in that you fill in every square based on local cost considerations. We call it *selective greed* because you explore many subproblems before combining the best of them to arrive at the optimal. It's a good metaphor for research.

Now it's your turn. You want to convert 'TAGATGGTCT' to 'TGGAGACAGTCT'. To get you started, I've given you the outline in Figure 2-11.

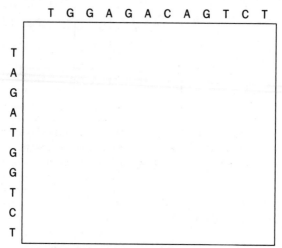

Figure 2-11: Fill in this matrix to solve the problem.

1. See if you can find the edit distance between the two strings by filling in the figure. While you're at it, count the different ways of converting 'TAGATGGTCT' to 'TGGAGACAGTCT'.

Solution to Selective Greed

1. See if you can find the edit distance between the two strings by filling in the figure. While you're at it, count the different ways of converting "TAGATG-GTCT" to "TGGAGACAGTCT".

Replace 'T' by 'T', insert 'G', insert 'G', replace 'A' by 'A', replace 'G' by 'G', replace 'A' by 'A', replace 'T' by 'C', replace 'G' by 'A', and then replace "GTCT" by "GTCT". This gives a total cost of 4, as shown in Figure 2-12.

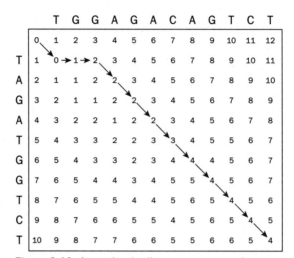

Figure 2-12: An optimal edit sequence to go from "TAGATGGTCT" to "TGGAGACAGTCT". Starting from the first letter, there are many replacements. Arrows always point to the right, downward, or to the right and downward.

Sweet Packs

A certain gourmet donut store prides itself on being able to provide its customers with any number of donuts between 1 and 160. A customer may go to the counter and say "I want 43 donuts" and 43 donuts will appear.

Warm-Up

The restaurant wants to package their donuts in four different sizes. Your job is to figure out what those sizes should be in order to minimize the number of packets needed to fill the average order. For starters, assume that any order between 1 and 160 is equally likely.

For example, suppose the packet sizes are 1, 5, 10, and 20. If a customer orders 48 donuts, then the number of packets required is six: two packets of 20, one of 5, and three of 1.

My recommended strategy is to try all possible different combinations of four sizes and find the best. A few observations make this fast. First, one of the sizes is constrained to be 1, so really you have to test ascending triplets of sizes between 2 and 160 only. When evaluating a triplet, include a packet of size 1, calculate the average cost, and simply keep the best.

The inner loop of this process is "calculate the average cost." That is, given a set of four packet sizes, compute the average number of packets needed for each order. Dynamic programming works really well for this purpose. See if you can figure out how.

Solution to Warm-Up

Here is high-level pseudo-code of one dynamic programming method.

Goal: Given four sizes 1, s1, s2, and s3, find the cost per order.

1. Create an array of size 160. This will be your cost array.

2. Initialize each entry to have infinite cost except for the entries at locations 1, s1, s2, and s3 to which you assign a cost of 1.

```
for entry i = 2 to 160
  if cost(i) == infinite
    for entry j from 1 to i-1
      if (cost(j) + cost(i-j)) < cost(i)
          cost(i) := (cost(j) + cost(i-j))
      end if
    end for
  end if
end for
```

3. Sum all the costs and divide by 160 to get the average cost.

This technique takes quadratic time in the maximum number of donuts, but this is fast enough for our purposes. Without using dynamic programming, one would have to work much harder.

Now that you see how to evaluate a given candidate set of packet sizes, it remains only to go through the different packet size triplet possibilities to find the best set of packet sizes.

1. Assuming orders for any number of donuts are equally likely, which set of packet sizes results in the minimum average number of packets required per order? What is that minimum average?

2. Assume that orders for any number of donuts under 50 are equally likely and are five times as likely as those over 50. So, for example, an order for 14 donuts is five times as likely as an order for 53 donuts, whereas it is equally likely to an order for 47 donuts. Which set of packet sizes gives the minimum average number of packets required per order in this case? What is that minimum average?

Solution to Sweet Packs

1. Assuming orders for any number of donuts are equally likely, which set of packet sizes gives the minimum average number of packets required per order? What is that minimum average?

The dynamic program given as part of the problem statement is the inner loop. The outer loop generates triplets, and then evaluates them. There are 4,019,679 triplets in all, but only 657,359 that are ascending. For each one, we evaluate the cost and try to find the minimum. This is admittedly not very cheap, but takes only a few minutes. The best set of packet sizes I could find was 1, 6, 29, and 37 having an average cost of 4.7 packets per request.

2. Assume that orders for any number of donuts under 50 are equally likely and are five times as likely as those over 50. So, for example, an order for 14 donuts is five times as likely as an order for 53 donuts, whereas it is equally likely to an order for 47 donuts. Which set of packet sizes gives the minimum average number of packets required per order in this case? What is that minimum average?

The same dynamic programming approach works, but the cost function has to change somewhat to reflect the change in likelihood. The way I did that was to multiply the cost of orders between 1 and 50 by five. To get the best average, divide the total cost by 360 (160 + (4 × 50)). Otherwise, nothing changes in the process. The best packet sizes are 1, 5, 12, and 32 and the average (weighted by likelihood) required number of packets is just under 4.

Revisiting a Traveling Salesman

The Traveling Salesman Problem, affectionately known as TSP, lies at the heart of many problems, including optimizing the deliveries of trucks, scheduling tour stops, and laying out wires. TSP yields very nicely to heuristics, but it also admits some beautiful theory.

A certain salesman, we'll call him Bob, starts at a certain city C and wants to visit a certain set of other cities by car at least once and then return to C. (*Factoid: What is the preferred profile of salespeople from pharmaceutical companies who call on doctors? Answer: Former cheerleaders.*) Travel times and costs may vary, but we will assume that the costs are positive, symmetric, and that the triangle inequality holds. Symmetry means that going from X to Y costs the same as going from Y to X. The triangle inequality means that going from X to Y to Z cannot be cheaper than going directly from X to Z (it could be the same price, but not cheaper).

The question is whether Bob can visit all his cities for a certain price or less. As you can see, if someone proposes a solution, you can verify that it meets the price budget easily, but finding a solution below a certain price can be hard—it may require exploring all possible paths.

Many people hear this problem and think: "Why can't a greedy approach work? That is, from each city, I'll just go to the next nearest one."

How bad can this get? That is, can you find a set of points where the greedy approach fails to find the minimum length route for the traveling salesman (assuming for the moment that cost is proportional to length)? Figure 2-13 lays out the visual for the problem.

Figure 2-13: The salesman starts at C and ends at C. Each time he goes to the closest unvisited city. How well will Bob do?

Using the greedy heuristic, if you start at point C, you will go down, right, up, right, down, right, up, right, down and then all the way back to C, as illustrated in Figure 2-14. In fact however, the best route would be to go directly right from C until the upper right hand point, then down, left and back to C, as in Figure 2-15.

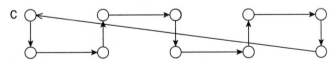

Figure 2-14: What happens when Bob visits the nearest previously unvisited city first?

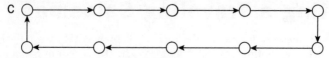

Figure 2-15: A better route for Bob.

When greed doesn't work, heuristics might help, but first there is the question of how bad greed could be. Concretely, can you find a situation, again assuming that cost is proportional to length, when the greedy "go to the next nearest city" strategy could be more than twice as costly as optimal?

I'm not going to answer this right away, because I want to present you with a strategy that is surely no more than twice as costly as optimal, is also greedy, and can easily be improved by heuristics. It also applies to every set of cities.

As you may already know, a *spanning tree* is a graph without cycles that connects all vertices (cities in our case). The cost of a spanning tree is the sum of the costs of its edges (remember that we assume that the cost to go from A to B is the same as the cost to go from B to A—symmetry). A minimum cost spanning tree is a spanning tree having the property that no other spanning tree has lower cost. To construct a minimum spanning tree starting at city C, we use the following algorithm:

```
Call an edge "useful" if it connects a vertex in a tree to a vertex
outside the tree.
 initialize the tree T to contain the city C and no edges
 until there are no more cities to include
     Add edge E to the edges of T if E is useful
         and for every other useful edge E'
         the cost of E' is greater than or equal to the cost of E
     Add the node of E not already in T to the nodes of T
 end until
```

Given the nodes in Figure 2-16, Figure 2-17 shows a minimum spanning tree (again where cost is proportional to distance).

Figure 2-16: A set of cities. Assume that cost is proportional to distance. The goal is to construct a minimum spanning tree.

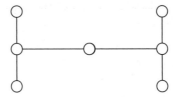

Figure 2-17: The minimum spanning tree in this case. Note that we do not need to know which is the starting city.

Now, here comes the key insight. The lowest cost route that a traveling salesman uses to visit all the cities is a spanning tree (though not necessarily a minimum cost one) if one ignores the final edge that brings the salesman back to his own city. The reason is that the route will touch all cities exactly once, because the triangle inequality makes it unprofitable to revisit a city. Because the route is a spanning tree (plus an extra edge), it must be at least as costly as the minimum spanning tree.

The consequence of this observation is that the cost of the minimum spanning tree provides a lower bound on the possible cost of the optimum traveling salesman route, *even if we never find that optimal route.*

We are not done, however. Every route is a spanning tree, but most minimum spanning trees are not routes. Fortunately, we can create a route from any minimum spanning tree that will never cost more than twice as much as the optimal route, as illustrated in Figure 2-18.

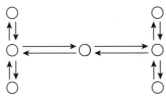

Figure 2-18: Take the minimum spanning tree and then go up and down each edge of the tree. That gives a route no matter which city one starts from. It's true that this route revisits cities, so can be improved. Already, though, its cost is no more than twice that of the optimal one.

Suppose we start at the center point and go right, then up, then down, down, then up, then left back to the center. We continue similarly on the left. The point is that every edge will be traversed twice. By symmetry, this means that the route costs twice as much as the minimum spanning tree. Because the minimum spanning tree is less expensive than the (unknown) optimal route, this route is less expensive than twice the cost of the optimal route.

Many improvements are now possible. Some are illustrated in Figure 2-19 where the returns to the center are done via diagonal lines. Beyond such heuristics, there are some guarantees. A very clever algorithm by N. Christofides showed that one could combine minimal matchings with spanning trees to obtain a route that is no more than 3/2 as expensive as the optimal one.

As clever as these approaches are, however, they don't necessarily extend to other problems, because they depend strongly on symmetry and the triangle inequality. Or do they?

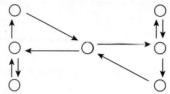

Figure 2-19: Some simple heuristic improvements to the minimum spanning tree-based route that will either leave the cost the same or reduce it (assuming the triangle inequality holds).

1. Can you find a case where, if symmetry and the triangle inequality do not hold, even the factor of two guarantee may not either? If not, can you prove that the spanning tree will always guarantee a cost that is no more than twice the optimal?

Solution to Revisiting a Traveling Salesman

1. Can you find a case where, if symmetry and the triangle inequality do not hold, even the factor of two guarantee may not either? If not, can you prove that the spanning tree will always guarantee a cost that is no more than twice the optimal?

When symmetry and the triangle inequality fail to hold, the spanning tree heuristic can be quite bad (see Figure 2-20).

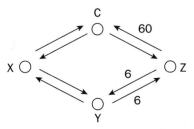

Figure 2-20: All unmarked edges have a cost of 5. The marked edge Z to C has a cost of 60 (violating symmetry and the triangle inequality). The marked edge Z to Y has a cost of 6, as does the edge from Y to Z.

Suppose that all edges have a cost of 5 except the three indicated. Then a spanning tree rooted at C will include the edges in Figure 2-21, because that is the least expensive tree starting from C in its construction phase. This gives a total cost of 85. By contrast, Figure 2-22 shows a tour that costs only 21.

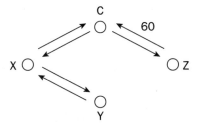

Figure 2-21: The spanning tree starting at C contains the directed edges C to Z, C to X, and C to Y. Back edges play no role. Unfortunately, the travel route using that tree must traverse the back edge having cost 60. Altogether we get a cost of 85.

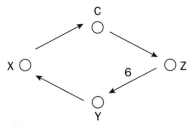

Figure 2-22: A much cheaper route moves clockwise through the nodes and has a cost of only 21.

Overloaded Scheduling and Freezing Crystals

When first faced with a problem, try pure greed (look for moves that lower the cost). If that doesn't work or if it reaches a dead end, then you can try case analysis as we did for Sudoko. If there are too many cases, then try dynamic programming. If all these fail, it is time for heuristic search techniques along with some bound on the optimum.

A heuristic technique is one that is not guaranteed to work perfectly, but often (you hope) works well. Greed is, of course, a great heuristic technique but can be brittle, as we saw in the solution to the "Finding a Schedule that Works" puzzle.

The principle of exploratory heuristic techniques is that they take anti-greedy moves sometimes. They do this in order to explore the search space. If each problem configuration could be encoded as some scalar value (horizontal axis of Figure 2-23), then the squiggly line in Figure 2-23 represents the cost of each configuration.

A greedy approach will make moves that decrease cost only. An exploratory heuristic technique will sometimes make moves to more costly states in the hopes of leaving a local minimum (see Figure 2-24). If this reminds you of high school chemistry notions of activation energy, you have the right intuition.

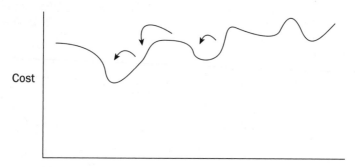

Some encoding of parameter options

Figure 2-23: The horizontal axis represents the search space. The vertical represents the cost. A greedy approach, given a location in the search space, will perform moves that decrease cost. So the arrows always start from a higher cost and go to a lower one.

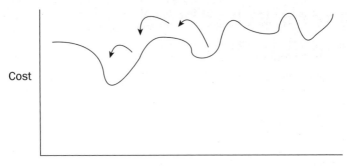

Some encoding of parameter options

Figure 2-24: In simulated annealing and other heuristic search techniques, some moves increase the cost. You can see that with the rightmost arrow which goes from a lower cost valley to a higher cost hill. The idea is to escape local cost minima.

But we don't want to go any which way all the time. Let's first look at animal analogies—flies vs. bees. If trying to leave the interior of a house, a fly, starting from a closed window, may bump against the window a few times, but will eventually fly away from that window and find an open one. Bees keep bumping up against the glass. Flies are using anti-greedy moves to escape the local optimum of the windowpane. Bees insist on trying to push through the pane.[2] On the other hand, flies never build anything as complex as a beehive. To me, this suggests that when you are faced with a technical problem, you must alternate between fly behavior and bee behavior. At some point you must stop exploring and start doing, but if you hit a roadblock, then you must start to explore some more.

The main exploratory search techniques are genetic (also known as evolutionary) algorithms, tabu searching, integer programming, and simulated annealing. A book that explains these techniques both engagingly and academically is *How to Solve It: Modern Heuristics* by Zvigniew Michalewicz and David B. Fogel (Springer, 2004).

Everybody seems to have a favorite. Mine is simulated annealing, because it requires fewer parameters than genetic algorithms and has a wider range of applicability than integer programming. I should note, however, that the other techniques work really well sometimes. If a problem is heavily numeric, for example, linear programming approximations to the integer programming problem can sometimes work well and avoid numerical inaccuracies. Some people make great use of genetic algorithms. I consider it a character flaw that I can't ever tune the parameters correctly.

---

[2]One can speculate that the reason people who make the most radical discoveries in science are young is that they act like flies. They are less committed to the methods that have worked in the past. Older people, like bees, make greedy moves hoping that experience will lead to an optimum result. To keep the edge, older folk should look around more.

Part II: The Secret of the Puzzle

Simulated annealing conforms to my intuition about the way the world works. I first heard about the technique in a lecture by its main inventor Kirkpatrick in 1983. He described how he had thought of the idea when he had to solve a traveling salesman-like problem — how to minimize the lengths of wires (I think power wires) around a circuit board. The problem was NP-complete but the company (IBM) needed a solution. Kirkpatrick was a solid-state physicist, so he suggested a technique inspired by the cooling of crystals.

If you take liquid silicon and freeze it quickly it will not form a crystal, which is the lowest energy state, but rather an amorphous (higher energy) blob. If you freeze it slowly ("anneal it"), then it will form a nice crystal. The slow cooling allows it to find an optimal state. At high temperatures atoms move rapidly, allowing them to escape local energy minima to fly off to far places. At lower temperatures, the atoms rearrange themselves only slightly.

Kirkpatrick reasoned that the same thing could be done with algorithms. Given a wire route at some stage of the algorithm, a move would replace, say, a random quadruple in the path, say A to B to C to D, by A to C to B to D in one of two cases:

❑ The change resulted in a shorter path.

❑ The change resulted in a longer path, but when you threw some pseudo-random dice, they came out in a certain improbable configuration.

Thus, step 2 is anti-greedy but occurs only with a certain probability. The key insight in Kirkpatrick's proposal was that this probability of taking an anti-greedy move would depend on both the amount by which the path became longer, and on the amount of time the algorithm had run. The probability would start out quite high (potentially near 1) but then gradually become lower as the algorithm proceeded. Towards the end, the algorithm almost never does anti-greedy moves. In annealing terms, the temperature decreases over the course of the algorithm as does the probability of taking anti-greedy moves. Here is the pseudo-code.

```
take an initial route r1
 initialize temperature T to a high value
 loop until T is low enough
     or you have found an answer close to optimal
   consider a randomly chosen possible change
           yielding a route r2
   if r2 is lower cost than r1
     then replace r1 by r2
     else replace r1 by r2 with probability
        e^((cost(r1)-cost(r2))/T)
   end if
   decrease the temperature T
 end loop
```

Note that the exponent is always negative for an anti-greedy move, so the probability is between 0 and 1. The larger the temperature T, the closer the exponent is to 0, so the higher the probability. Also, the larger the increase in cost the more negative, so the lower the probability. Thus, anti-greed tends to happen earlier and for small increases in cost.

Now, Kirkpatrick observed that the technique was in no way dependent on the specifics of wire layout, as I hope you can see from the pseudo-code. Further, the only parameters are the initial temperature, the speed at which the temperature decreases, and an encoding of the cost.

The elegance of this approach immediately appealed to me, but the feeling was not universal. One professor asked pointedly, "What have you proved?" "Nothing," Kirkpatrick replied with that impatience that physicists manifest when faced with questions from pesky mathematicians. "Under certain conditions one can show that if you freeze infinitely slowly you will get a crystal, but what this means in terms of an algorithm is very uncertain."

Their exchange illustrates a cultural divide between the heurist and the algorithmist. The heurist has an NP-hard problem to solve, so uses a heuristic that seems at least plausible. The algorithmist wants a time guarantee. Both have their place, but since NP-completeness has been around since the 1970s and no algorithm seems to be coming over the horizon, it's possible that we'll be stuck with heuristics for quite some time for many problems.

Heuristic search techniques offer no guarantee, however. The search space could have just one sweet spot protected by a high-cost slope as in Figure 2-25. This would make it hard even for simulated annealing to find the optimum.

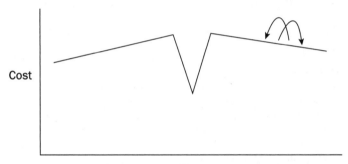

Some encoding of parameter options

Figure 2-25: A search space for which simulated annealing might have a difficult time finding a solution. The optimum is at a very specific part of the search space, so a move is unlikely to find it.

I invite you now to apply simulated annealing to the overloaded scheduling problem. Here is how it goes. You have a bunch of tasks, each of which has a deadline, an amount of work, and a positive value. You receive all the value of the task if you finish by the deadline and nothing if you finish after the deadline. You have more work to do than you could possibly finish.

Task T1 takes 3 days with deadline on day 19 and value 17

Task T2 takes 4 days with deadline on day 23 and value 14

Task T3 takes 6 days with deadline on day 51 and value 10

Task T4 takes 3 days with deadline on day 30 and value 7

Task T5 takes 7 days with deadline on day 38 and value 13

Task T6 takes 6 days with deadline on day 36 and value 11

Task T7 takes 7 days with deadline on day 45 and value 18

Task T8 takes 3 days with deadline on day 16 and value 10

Task T9 takes 5 days with deadline on day 22 and value 13

Task T10 takes 2 days with deadline on day 13 and value 16

Task T11 takes 8 days with deadline on day 12 and value 6

Task T12 takes 1 day with deadline on day 31 and value 15

Task T13 takes 5 days with deadline on day 17 and value 13

Task T14 takes 2 days with deadline on day 2 and value 13

Task T15 takes 7 days with deadline on day 30 and value 11

Task T16 takes 5 days with deadline on day 11 and value 18

Task T17 takes 4 days with deadline on day 4 and value 10

Task T18 takes 5 days with deadline on day 27 and value 15

Task T19 takes 4 days with deadline on day 6 and value 15

1. How much value can you obtain in total from these tasks?

Now, before attempting to answer this using simulated annealing (or any technique of your choice), first try to establish an upper bound on the value. A simple upper bound is the sum of all values. But such an upper bound might be excessively high. So, let's consider another method. Define the value density of a task to be the value of the task divided by the number of days it takes. For example, T18 has a value density of 15/5 = 3. Now, take the highest deadline (51 in this case). Order the tasks by descending order of their value densities.

```
T12: 15
T10: 8
T14: 6.5
T1: 5.666667
T19: 3.75
T16: 3.6
T2: 3.5
T8: 3.333333
T18: 3
T9: 2.6
T13: 2.6
T7: 2.571429
T17: 2.5
T4: 2.333333
T5: 1.857143
T6: 1.833333
T3: 1.666667
T15: 1.571429
T11: 0.75
```

To compute the upper bound, note their computation time and see how many of these tasks starting from the one with highest value density can complete by day 51. If there is any time left over, then use the next task's value density and multiply it by the number of days left.

In this case, we can complete all tasks down to task T17 in 50 days using the value density ordering. The upper bound, therefore, is the total value for tasks T12, T10, T14, T1, T19, T16, T2, T8, T18, T9, T13, T7, T17, which is 187 plus the value density of T4 times the one day remaining (2.3). The total, therefore, is 189.3. Now this upper bound is generous in that we have loosely assumed that all these tasks have deadline 51. But it may still be useful.

Also, the value density heuristic may yield a good starting configuration for simulated annealing. Okay, enough hints. Try it for yourself.

Solution to Overloaded Scheduling and Freezing Crystals

1. **How much value can you obtain in total from these tasks?**

We'll follow the heuristic of preferring tasks with the greatest value density (value/computation time), suggesting a schedule of T14 T19 T16 T10 T8 T1 T2 T15 T12 T5 T7 T3. These give values of 13, 15, 18, 16, 10, 17, 14, 11, 15, 13, 18, and 10 respectively for a total of 170. That is quite close to the upper bound of 183. See if you can anneal to something better.

Wordsnakes

Real-world problems related to the Traveling Salesman Problem often introduce considerations that make the situation far more difficult. For example, it is easy to imagine that price considerations may have to be balanced against salesman morale, customer availability, and market conditions if a real salesman were at issue. But even staying with simple cost functions, symmetry and the triangle inequality may not hold.

What carries over are:

1. The desire to estimate bounds (i.e. what is the optimal conceivable solution), because that will tell you whether it is worth struggling for more improvements.

2. Heuristic problem solving techniques.

As an illustration, consider a problem that can be formulated similarly to the Traveling Salesman Problem but requires new analysis.

Given a set of words, a wordsnake is a string containing all the words in the set. The optimal wordsnake is the one of shortest length. For example, given the words "super" and "perfect," two possible wordsnakes are "superfect" or "perfectsuper." The first one is shorter, so is better. Your problem is to find an optimal (shortest) wordsnake covering a set of words, given that you are allowed to rearrange the words.

Here are the words:

subway

dentist

wayward

highway

terrible

english

less

blessed

warden

rib

stash

shunt

hunter

Part II: The Secret of the Puzzle

What does this have to do with Traveling Salesman? Well, let's look at edges between pairs of words, for example, "warden" → "english." We will consider the cost of this edge to be the number of letters of the target word ("english" in this case) that will be needed in the wordsnake that combines these two in this order (i.e., beyond those letters also included in "warden"). For this edge, the wordsnake would have "wardenglish," so the cost of this edge is the length of "glish" or 5. Note that the edge "english" → "warden" has a cost of 6 (the full length of "warden"). So symmetry need not hold (though the triangle inequality does).

What would be a good lower bound on the length of the optimal wordsnake? Please pause to consider this before you read on.

I would vote for the following: For each word, consider all edges having that word as target. Find the edge having the smallest cost and add up all such smallest costs. For example, consider "shunt." The lowest cost edge having "shunt" as a target is "stash" → "shunt" at a cost of 3. So associate 3 with "shunt." Now just add all the associated costs with each word and you have an approximate lower bound to the cost. (It's approximate because it's conceivable that a word could be found in a partly constructed wordsnake. For example, if the words were "shunt," "stash," "till," and "until," then the wordsnake stashuntill would contain "until" even though the lowest cost edge from any single word to "until" has a cost of two.)

1. How close can you come to this approximate optimal for these words?

Solution to Wordsnakes

1.   How close can you come to this approximate optimal for these words?

Order the words as follows (according to their best edges) and see that you come very close to the lower bound.

subway

wayward

warden

english

shunt

hunter

terrible

rib

blessed

less

dentist

stash

highway

Here is the corresponding wordsnake:

```
subwaywardenglishunterriblessedentistashighway
```

Maximal Friends

Achieving a factor of two of the optimal seems to happen often in computational problems. As in the Traveling Salesman Problem, this problem uses a setting involving roads, but with a strong xenophobic bite.

Imagine a set of city-states. There are roads connecting some of them and it's possible to travel from any city to any other, though the trip may require some intermediate stops. There may be several routes between two cities, i.e., the roads need not constitute a spanning tree. All roads are two-way.

We say two cities are neighbors if there is a road connecting them. Cities make alliances only with neighbors. Further, no city makes more than one alliance. If cities A and B are allied, we will call them *matched*. A maximal matching occurs when every city C is either matched or all neighbors of C are matched with other cities.

Warm-Up

Suppose there are eight cities. How few matches could there be in a maximal matching?

Solution to Warm-Up

There could be just one, represented here by the solid line segment in Figure 2-26.

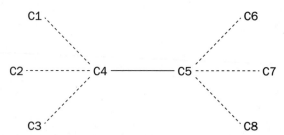

Figure 2-26: Each line segment (dashed or solid) represents a road. The solid line represents an alliance. Only C4 and C5 are matched. No other city has an ally.

That single matching precludes all others and therefore is maximal. At this point, let me remind you of the difference between maximal and maximum: a *maximal* state is one to which you can add nothing, in this case more matchings. Maximum means you cannot get a larger number. So this matching is maximal, but it doesn't give the maximum number of possible matches of any maximal matching. That honor belongs to the matching in Figure 2-27 (among many other symmetrically constructed ones).

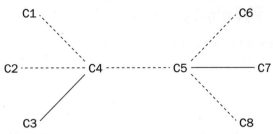

Figure 2-27: In this case, we have two matchings: C3 with C4, and C5 with C7. Other pairs of cities could be matched, but there cannot be more than two matching pairs in all.

The warm-up shows that the poor maximal matching of the first figure had half the number of matches as the one in the second figure. One might wonder how general an observation that is.

1.   Is there any configuration of cities and roads for which the maximum maximal matching has more than twice as many matches as some other maximal matching? If so, show it. Otherwise, prove that this cannot happen.

Part II: The Secret of the Puzzle

Solution to Maximal Friends

1. **Is there any configuration of cities and roads for which the maximum maximal matching has more than twice as many matches as some other maximal matching? If so, show it. Otherwise, prove that this cannot happen.**

It cannot happen. That is, the maximum maximal matching (let's call it Mmax) cannot have more than twice the number of matches than even the worst maximal matching (let's call that one Mbad). The reason is simple. Consider an edge in Mbad between nodes n1 and n2. Eliminating that edge makes n1 and n2 available to match other nodes, but n1 can match only one other node and similarly for n2. So eliminating the edge between n1 and n2 can do no more than make two other edges possible.

Winning at the Slots

Heuristics help to move through a search space based on cost and perhaps enlightened greed (as in simulated annealing). Sometimes you don't control the size of the search space, however, or there are winning configurations and losing configurations and nothing in between. In such cases, you might still do better than a brute force exhaustive search if there is structure in the winning configurations.

A field known as *combinatorial design* can help. The idea is that even if you don't test the full search space, perhaps you can be systematic in some sense at least. For example, perhaps you can guarantee that every value of every parameter is tried at least once. Usually, that's insufficient. Perhaps you can ensure that every combination of values of every pair of parameters is tried once. In this puzzle, we look for triplets.

Consider a special slot machine with five wheels. One has four different values. The others have three each.

> wheel 1: apples, cherries, grapes, pears
>
> wheel 2: cherries, grapes, pears
>
> wheel 3: apples, grapes, pears
>
> wheel 4: apples, cherries, pears
>
> wheel 5: apples, cherries, grapes

In this machine, the player sets the wheel values, then pulls the lever. If it's a winning combination, the payout is $500. Each pull of the lever costs $10. The winning combination depends on only three wheels. You don't know which three, but you know that the first wheel is one of them. If you are lucky enough to find the correct values of the correct three wheels, the values in the remaining two wheels don't matter. For example, suppose the winning combination is apples on wheel 1, grapes on wheel 3, and pears on wheel 4. If you set those values correctly, then the values on wheels 2 and 5 can be anything at all and you will receive the payout.

Warm-Up

 The house changes the winning combinations after either 15 attempts or a payout, whichever comes first. If each attempt costs $10 and the payout is $500, can you make this into a good game for the player?

Solution to Warm-Up

In order to understand how to go about solving this problem, realize first that there are nine winning combinations since there are nine possible settings of the remaining wheels. The total number of combinations of all wheels is $4 \times 3 \times 3 \times 3 \times 3 = 324$. So the odds of winning are $9/324 = 1/36$. Because each pull of the lever costs $10 and the payout is $500, this is a good bet. That would be true even if the winning combination were changed after every attempt.

In fact, the odds are better than this, because each attempt reduces the search space. This increases the odds just as your chances of winning increase as the deck empties in black jack, if you keep track of the cards thrown.

1. Can you show how to guarantee to win in 36 lever pulls?

Notice that you want to combine each value of wheel 1 with every pair of values of every pairs of other wheels. For example, if the order of these fruits correspond to wheel numbers, then the three lever pulls

> 1,apples,pears,apples,pears,apples
>
> 2,apples,cherries,apples,apples,grapes
>
> 3,apples,grapes,apples,cherries,cherries

correspond to setting apples for wheel 1 and then testing all other wheels against apples for wheel 3. At the same time, we have tested pears vs. pears, cherries vs. apples, and grapes vs. cherries for wheels 2 and 4. So, for each setting of wheel 1, we can test many wheel-to-wheel pairs of the other wheels with just a few lever pulls. Keep track of value pairs that haven't yet been tried and go through them systematically. That's enough of a hint. You can program this.

Solution to Winning at the Slots

1. **Can you show how to guarantee to win in 36 lever pulls?**

Here are the 36 lever pulls that will guarantee that every possible value of the first wheel is combined with every pair of values from each pair of other wheels.

num	wheel1	wheel2	wheel3	wheel4	wheel5
1	apples	pears	apples	pears	apples
2	apples	cherries	apples	apples	grapes
3	apples	grapes	apples	cherries	cherries
4	apples	cherries	grapes	cherries	apples
5	apples	pears	pears	cherries	grapes
6	apples	cherries	pears	pears	cherries
7	apples	pears	grapes	apples	cherries
8	apples	grapes	pears	apples	apples
9	apples	grapes	grapes	pears	grapes
10	cherries	pears	apples	pears	apples
11	cherries	cherries	apples	apples	grapes
12	cherries	grapes	apples	cherries	cherries
13	cherries	cherries	grapes	cherries	apples
14	cherries	pears	pears	cherries	grapes
15	cherries	cherries	pears	pears	cherries
16	cherries	pears	grapes	apples	cherries
17	cherries	grapes	pears	apples	apples
18	cherries	grapes	grapes	pears	grapes

num	wheel1	wheel2	wheel3	wheel4	wheel5
19	grapes	pears	apples	pears	apples
20	grapes	cherries	apples	apples	grapes
21	grapes	grapes	apples	cherries	cherries
22	grapes	cherries	grapes	cherries	apples
23	grapes	pears	pears	cherries	grapes
24	grapes	cherries	pears	pears	cherries
25	grapes	pears	grapes	apples	cherries
26	grapes	grapes	pears	apples	apples
27	grapes	grapes	grapes	pears	grapes
28	pears	pears	apples	pears	apples
29	pears	cherries	apples	apples	grapes
30	pears	grapes	apples	cherries	cherries
31	pears	cherries	grapes	cherries	apples
32	pears	pears	pears	cherries	grapes
33	pears	cherries	pears	pears	cherries
34	pears	pears	grapes	apples	cherries
35	pears	grapes	pears	apples	apples
36	pears	grapes	grapes	pears	grapes

Understanding Dice

If you find probability analyses to be challenging, you are not alone. Many people find that their intuition can lead to errors when faced with a complicated scenario involving probabilities.

In this, I may be a typical specimen. Between the ages of 8 and 11, I spent beautiful afternoons, well, inside. Specifically, I gambled — black jack, roulette, but above all poker. Antes were 3 cents, so winning $5 was an amazing day. Usually, I won. I rarely bluffed and I had an experiential feel for the probabilities of different hands.

This intuition worked well for simple problems, but I lacked analytical tools. Courses on probability helped, but I found it very easy to make seemingly small mistakes that could lead to large errors.

It seems that even professional mathematicians are not immune. In 1990, the columnist Marilyn vos Savant published a puzzle called the Monty Hall problem. Even though she gave the right answer, many people, including mathematicians, told her she was wrong. Here is how the puzzle goes. Let's see how you do.

A game show host, Monty Hall, always follows the same protocol. He shows three doors, D1, D2, and D3, to a contestant. Behind one is a valuable gift and Monty knows which one. The other doors have gags. The contestant chooses a door, say D1. Monty doesn't open the door, but opens another door D2 that has a gag gift. Monty offers the contestant a choice to switch from D1 to the third door D3. Now, the question is: Should the contestant switch or not?

To analyze the situation, start by listing all configurations that have equal probabilities. Then analyze the choice for the contestant in each case. Here, V means a valuable gift and G means a gag gift.

D1	D2	D3
V	G	G
G	V	G
G	G	V

If the contestant chooses the correct door to begin with, he wins by not switching. However, in the two other cases, he wins by switching. That is, in two out of three cases, switching is better. So, the contestant should switch. It's as easy as that.

The strategy of writing down all the equi-probable configurations works in lots of situations. Let's try a few more.

 A challenger, Alice, throws a pair of fair dice, keeps them under an opaque cup and peeks at them. She tells you the total of the pair is 6. She offers you an even money bet: Tell me the maximum die value and I'll pay you $100. Otherwise, you pay me $100. Do you take it?

Write down the configurations that have the equal probabilities.

5	1
4	2
3	3
2	4
1	5

As you can see, two out of five times, the maximum value is 5. Two out of five times, the maximum value is 4. One out of five times, the maximum value is 3. The probability of winning is too low for an even money payout. You should not take the bet.

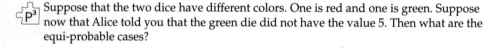 Now she tells you that neither die is 5. She still offers you the same bet. Do you take it now?

At this point there are three equi-probable cases:

4	2
3	3
2	4

So, now you guess 4 and will win two times out of three.

Suppose that the two dice have different colors. One is red and one is green. Suppose now that Alice told you that the green die did not have the value 5. Then what are the equi-probable cases?

Green	Red
4	2
3	3
2	4
1	5

Now, if you choose 4, your chances of winning are exactly 1/2.

Here is a harder one:

1. Suppose that the green die is unfair. In fact it has a 1/2 chance of being 3 and a 1/10 chance of being any other value. The red die is fair. Alice rolls an 8. She again offers you an even money bet to choose the maximum die value. Do you take it?

Solution to Understanding Dice

1. Suppose that the green die is unfair. In fact it has a 1/2 chance of being 3 and a 1/10 chance of being any other value. The red die is fair. Alice rolls an 8. She again offers you an even money bet to choose the maximum die value. Do you take it?

Again, create a table of equi-probable situations. In this case, we will start with the equi-probable situations including those that don't lead to 8.

Green	Red
1	1, 2, 3, 4, 5, 6
2	1, 2, 3, 4, 5, 6
3	1, 2, 3, 4, 5, 6
3	1, 2, 3, 4, 5, 6
3	1, 2, 3, 4, 5, 6
3	1, 2, 3, 4, 5, 6
3	1, 2, 3, 4, 5, 6
4	1, 2, 3, 4, 5, 6
5	1, 2, 3, 4, 5, 6
6	1, 2, 3, 4, 5, 6

We represented 3 five times because it is five times as likely as the other green values, which are all equally likely. Now cross out those configurations that are impossible because we know the total is 8. That leaves the following:

Green	Red
2	6
3	5
3	5
3	5
3	5
3	5
4	4
5	3
6	2

In six of these nine cases, 5 is the maximum value. So your chances of winning are $6/9 = 2/3$.

Bait and Switch

A new game show with doors has been invented and you are invited. In this case, there are two doors. Each has a pile of gold Krugerrands behind it, but one has twice as many as the other. You point to a door. The game show host opens it for you, then offers to allow you to switch your choice.

Picture it. You are on stage, the TV lights glaring. The host has just opened the door. Before you lie the coins, glistening. The audience lets out a moan of admiration and envy. For a moment you feel faint. Then the game show host, Monty Hall style, interrupts your reverie and offers you the opportunity to switch doors. (He does this to every contestant every time.) Do you do it?

Before you decide, you have to know the possibilities. Half the time, there are 100 coins behind one door and 200 coins behind the other. One quarter of the time there are 200 behind one door and 400 behind the other. One quarter of the time there are 400 coins behind one door and 800 behind the other.

You want to maximize your expected winnings.

Warm-Up

Suppose you see 100 coins behind your initially chosen door. Would you switch then?

Solution to Warm-Up

Duh. Clearly yes, because you cannot lose. If there are 800 coins, just as clearly you don't change.

---

1. Would you switch if you see 200 coins behind the door?
2. Would you switch if you see 400 coins behind the door?
3. Suppose that the probabilities were 1/3, 1/3, 1/3 instead of 1/2, 1/4, 1/4. Then would you switch if there were 400 coins?

It's a new season and the game show producers are afraid of a drop of popularity. For that reason the producers set the range of coins to be much larger: 25, 50, 100, 200, 400, 800, 1600, 3200, and 6400. All the door possibilities—25-50, 50-100, and so on up to 3200-6400—are equally likely.

4. Assuming your first selected door opens to any number of coins other than 25 or 6,400, should you switch?

Another season passes and the TV ratings are flagging just a little. The producer decides to extend the range from 1 coin to 1,048,576 coins. All x-and-2x possibilities are equally likely, he promises. But now that the extremes are so unlikely, the host won't bother opening the door that the contestant first guesses. When the contestant makes his final choice, the curtain opens to a large bucket of gold, the sight of which causes predictable shrieks among the audience.

5. Should the contestant switch even when the host doesn't open the contestant's initial door?

Solution to Bait and Switch

1.   Would you switch if you see 200 coins behind the door?

Let's find the equi-probable events. Because the 100-200 situation is twice as likely as any other, we'll write that one twice. The following are the equi-probable door pair situations:

100	200
100	200
200	400
400	800

Therefore, if you see 200 coins, you are twice as likely to be in the 100-200 situation as in any other. Switching to the other door, therefore, is twice as likely to cause you to lose 100 coins as to win 200. So, your expected winning by switching is zero. It's your call.

2.   Would you switch if you see 400 coins behind the door?

In this case, you are as likely to be in the 200-400 as in the 400-800 situation. In the first case, switching costs you 200 coins. In the second, switching enables you to win 400. So you expect to benefit by switching.

3.   Suppose that the probabilities were 1/3, 1/3, 1/3 instead of 1/2, 1/4, 1/4. Then would you switch if there were 400 coins?

In this case, the equi-probable situations are:

100	200
200	400
400	800

Nothing has changed for the 400 coin case — you should switch. By the way, you should switch in the 200 coin case as well. Half the time, you'll win an extra 200 coins.

4.   Assuming your first selected door opens to any number of coins other than 25 or 6,400, should you switch?

Switch every time. It's the same reasoning as in question 3.

5. **Should the contestant switch even when the host doesn't open the door to which the contestant first points?**

Switching doesn't help on the average. By symmetry it can't. If it did, then the contestant could have simply chosen the other door to begin with. As the game show host opened no door, the contestant has gained no information. But how do we show this analytically? The equi-probable situations are:

1	2
2	4
4	8
...	
524,288	1,048,576

In each case, if the contestant switches in one direction in the x-and-2x situation he will win x; if he switches in the other, he will lose x. So switching as a strategy yields no net gain (or loss). Why is this protocol different from the one where the host opens the door that the contestant first points to? In that protocol, the only time the contestant doesn't switch is when he sees the bucket with 1,048,576 coins. That happens only one time in 40, but in that case, the contestant saves 524,288 coins by not switching. Therein lies the contestant's edge.

Part III
Faithful Foes

A gentle hand may lead an elephant by a hair.
— Persian proverb

Part III: Faithful Foes

The high-speed train from Montpellier to Paris hurtled through the French countryside at 300 kilometers per hour, but to Ecco and me this seemed way too slow. Ecco still held a tight grip on the note our bed and breakfast hostess had given us that morning — the message from Kate: "Jake, come to Paris immediately. Don't call. Rose has disappeared."

The vacation had started so well. Ecco and his French windsurfing pals had jumped the waves off Gruissan the day before. We spent the evening at the casino in town listening to a pair of beautiful folk singers. Ecco had planned to sleep late, because the best winds come up in the afternoon, but we were awakened by a loud knock on the door. "Monsieur Ecco, please wake yourself up," our hostess had said. "The woman Kate has left you a message."

Now we were on the train and Ecco had said hardly a word for the last hour. I, too, was deep in thought. Everything seemed so mysterious about this affair. For starters, why wouldn't Kate want us to call?

"She might think her phone line is tapped, Professor," Ecco said, apparently sensing my thoughts. "She doesn't want her daughter put in unnecessary danger. Rose has been climbing with her closest friends, so she wouldn't disappear on her own accord. Someone has done this to her."

"Has she been kidnapped?" I asked.

"That's not the worst possibility," Ecco replied. "We'll know more once we see Kate and the others."

Ecco fell silent again and I reviewed what I knew of Rose's life to see if I could figure out who would want to do her harm. Unfortunately, the suspects were all too evident. Kate had raised Rose along the Columbia River near Hood River, Oregon. After Ecco and Kate met, Kate took up windsurfing and she taught her then 12-year-old daughter Rose. Rose's agility made her a natural for fun boarding and she spent many days on the water, winning many competitions along the way. But Rose's first love was rock climbing. From Smith Rock to Beacon and on to eastern Washington, Kate knew the best spots and the best climbers.

When Rose was 17, Kate moved the family consisting of Rose and her younger twin siblings Cloe and Eli to Dayton, Ohio, for work reasons. Rose went to art school in Cleveland, turning her energy to architectural sculpture, and when she needed some money, into social work. Homeless kids, problem kids, any kid in trouble — Rose worked with them all. She built shelters with them, found homes for them, and talked with them. They confided everything to her. One of her young friends was Dumpster diving shortly after the November 2004 elections and found a bag full of punched ballots from Cuyahoga County. Rose suspected foul play and kept them.

For her safety's sake, that may not have been wise. No longer could she play the free student; she was now on the run, pursued by a shadowy group of religious fanatics who had taken the name Warriors of the Rapture and used as their symbol a red cross rising from a blazing fire. They followed her back to Oregon, severely roughing up her climbing friend

Scot. They wanted the ballots; that much was clear. Rose hid them under a tree. A little while later, when she and another friend were driving over the Hood River bridge, they were trapped between two pickup trucks. Rose guessed what might happen if she were caught, and jumped off the bridge. Against all odds, she survived the jump and swam to safety. While she was in hiding, Kate, Ecco, and an assortment of helpers managed to bring the ballots to light and prove they were authentic, thereby uncovering the greatest election fraud in the history of the republic. (For the full story, see my chronicles in *Puzzler's Elusion.*) Core members of the Warriors of the Rapture were caught laying explosives and were put away. That was the end of the affair, or so we thought.

Our problems began with the question of fame. Whereas most people seem to crave it, Dr. Ecco shunned the spotlight. "This has been my second brief descent into notoriety and I hope it's my last," he told me shortly after the last of the big cheese Warriors was caught. "I want to return to what I do best — solve puzzles in the safety of my living room."

Fame has a way of changing business as usual, however. People deal with you differently and sometimes you don't know why. In Ecco's case, celebrities called on him endlessly concerning their pressing personal problems. More or less patiently, Ecco would explain that his profession of "omniheurism" was not as omni as they hoped. "The problems I solve must be of a mathematical nature. I can't tell you which hair color will get you the next acting role."

Besides celebrities, government agencies still came to call, but often with bug sweepers and white-noise makers. Even with that, they spoke in voices barely louder than whispers.

The glare of publicity disturbed his tranquility, but he admitted its benefits. "A little fame helps in airports and restaurants," he mentioned to me one day after we had managed to swing a late reservation at his favorite restaurant, Il Molino.

Then, about three months ago, the letters started. It was the first Saturday of June. Someone slipped a letter into Ecco's New York City mailbox. The single page inside had the words "Babylon Falls" emblazoned in black over an image of a rampaging fire. The fire image differed from the one of the Warriors of the Rapture. That one looked demure by comparison. This resembled the fire of a firestorm.

Three weeks after that, I found another note crumpled in front of Ecco's door. I could see the same fire image in the background, but the words were different: "And upon her forehead was a name written..."

Ecco took a look when I handed it to him, turning the paper one way and the other as he walked around his living room.

"Why all these phrases from the Bible? It might be some kind of taunt, but why?" Ecco asked these questions aloud, but neither of us had any clue as to answers.

Another two weeks passed. A flier was pasted to Ecco's door. Same fire motif and the words: "And a mighty angel took up a stone, a millstone, and cast it into the sea."

Ecco looked up the phrase in the Bible and saw that in the context of Revelation, it too spoke about violence to the city of Babylon.

Part III: Faithful Foes

"Suppose it's a warning, Professor Scarlet," Ecco said to me. "It could be a warning about New York, which some fundamentalists liken to a sinful Babylon. Still, the reference to a woman could mean something else. Didn't Rose say she was going with her friend Scot to climb at Fontainebleau near Paris? It's early autumn. The windsurfing should be great around Port Leucat. Maybe I should invite Kate along for the ride and suggest that Rose invite lots of friends."

"May I join you?" I asked. "I'm on sabbatical this semester."

"Yes, I would like that very much," Ecco replied.

We arrived in France in mid-September. Kate stayed in Paris. Rose and her friends camped at Fontainebleau. Ecco and I headed to the Mediterranean. Ecco, the thinker, the solver of puzzles of remarkable difficulty, seemed completely at home during those first several days with wind speeds of 65 kilometers per hour. Wind and water — so refreshing, so direct, so innocent. Ecco is right to love them, I thought. People are evolutionarily adapted to face the elements, not kidnappers and violence to one's friends. But now here we were: Rose was gone. I could only hope she was safe.

"Jake and Professor Scarlet, I'm so glad you're here," Kate said as Ecco and I lay our knapsacks down in the well-appointed apartment. In appreciation for Ecco's previous services for the French government, Yves Maison had put at our disposal a spacious penthouse apartment overlooking the Seine and the Citroën Park. Kate had been there for the week, and bags from various boutiques showed she had not been idle.

"She's gone," Kate said, looking at us both. I had never seen her look so pale. "Rose has disappeared. All I have is an envelope addressed to us in her handwriting. Inside there is a typed letter that appears to be in code with a Sudoku inside it. Each of Rose's friends also has been sent to a different spot here in Paris to copy an encoded inscription. They're waiting to talk to you. But first, look at the letter from Rose."

```
Efbs Oqo, Ghdu Hv. Jhht,

O'Bk hzrlk uG ljyCxAB GroDroB T oAGxp JEvGr o AtIItG. jxuO Jrzu LzsL BM QuM
JF, xQP f FyB SN TAKE QSFDBVUJPOT WR EZSMH NYX LGRROTM PU bPM faXWP RKXNc.
Ea gURl gOWR iWTn mekbT VeTipgk al TYmXk C rmjoZ ep. Fc wms'tc qdZc this
gbs, kv'u suredeoB so.

Knwxy EuA ohCl Bw twxF DrkD T Ftuzw V'z uCwBu ID ru FB. lzwQ PBEE NuEy Hz
wSwU yRQ LMR ENQ TOO MPOH. vJGa WROG QI YMJd cUT'Z OHYT UM RW KXi hLj. u
Qba'g Ybck lWTgT y'c XfZeX WalZWj, Unm C Yj dWra pljb gldmpkYrgml.

Rdbnmc, I lopx yjgtg pB jvmirhw Bjwj yktz: Nhyl UwvBxizviAAm, QkBo op
XKAz, cynpr XsoBBs s'PGr, gFIKv v'gJDwsFK, iEtvx xy Gv XwOPEHHA, mIxzB BC
Kz nATION, mF uGPCV, jDUH h'eYWXIVPMXd, FSI, TGZaXGRRe p OcMaa, oQVScO
yZecP pMYQ.

GUVeQ, hVSm'jS idaS cU kYRk qgm pbee VY VWgZ pk cfka kc sgqntfg an fousbodf
kp d givxemr ymjfywj Ckrr luvBno. bpmG'zm wxC Dyy nwplC mnAGF GuvF HvsoHFs
```

xC vqsJ. Z'D FGL LNKx QByNByL DO'N OPEHH xzQFSB MP MNS BUT UIFZ UCa LW'V
SPH, NY aYKJ aV aMIb cQXdbJWMb, KXN XLYj aR gUR dSfTcfaObQSg RdcRTgcTS
mQjUh ReU VWSlZ. LhngWl mjiies.

Ajpm, pdau pXfa rfc knbZshnm of uijt vjgcvtg lv ettvsBmqexipC ymj iktzkx
(AolF Aiql "Cqn lkvkxmo AztyE") Ar FrIrA Ct Iwt IyJuI KF OzAuz FR zLCyHxM
RzMz OAJP. tEFzE QCTCL? gDQD IS XIBU VJGa VDLG: "wYTTSWI dTZ IGT VYKLY bPM
bcXaRNb SX eSP YQeeMSQe lbhe TfWSbRg WPkT hUSUYlUT, ReU fmeTWj maXf 1
ocmjpbc 9 XZZloafkd rm sgZs order. Pqy khuh mw f yAjuqA.

7							6	4
		6						
					8		2	
5	6	3						
				7		2		9
	5					3		
			4				9	
1	7		9					8

Tjp'gg jkpeYa qeb qgvrf khmd is bmm 0u (0v gsvviwtsrh yt hrgtqy). dolu GwC
BxuEn DrsC DFozvF, xAAw nG Hvs uxGHI IuLuD ELDsvIJ AF MAtM FCHy. oCzMz
IECDP yB y EDV SOLUTIONS. jG UQ, NQRZ XLEX YMJ cUSKT OHcL JMMV bNWc dY
cPWPgLYe XaOMfUaZe. sVTheR cih iWT beSQjYedi TfiiVjgfeUZeX lg mahlX
hogVYlm amjh pda jbppXdbp. Dglb sgd balance qpjou. aqw zloo fi hqtxj zu
Aol BCvvmt nwCAjwln."

S ozy'E wzAI nAL ACFs IwpC JxqJ. gCvrJv uGEw yBGw Gy, vN OKKJ xP WMS BzM. i
TBZ VJCV l XVYWX YMJR, HaZ UVa bPIb VdLQ. (sP eSPj fdMZeXMfQ gUNg ZWbS,
Xi'h Q XffU kaYf.)

EhoX, LimY

"Do you think she is still alive?" Kate asked Ecco after he put the letter down a minute later. I didn't see how Ecco could answer, as I could make nothing of the letter.

"I think so," Ecco said. "It would have been easy enough to kill her; a sniper's bullet in the Fontainebleau woods when Rose and her friends were climbing would have done the deed. So, I think she's physically okay."

I wanted to believe Ecco, but I felt as worried as Kate. Ecco turned to me.

"My dear Professor," he said to me. "Rose disappears. Her friends return. Whoever wanted Rose may have simply wanted to talk to her alone. They even let her write a letter."

"Couldn't they have just said they needed privacy?" I thought, but decided not to speak.

Ecco may have guessed my question because he flashed a brief smile and nodded, but instead he turned to Kate and said, "Let's now go hear from Rose's climbing friends." We walked into the large dining room where they had been waiting.

Amalea, a writer when she wasn't climbing, was the first to speak up.

"We camped in the forest of Fontainebleau, near a little town called Milly," Amalea began. "It's ideal for climbing. The trees offer lots of cover when it's hot, but most boulders are partly exposed to the sun, so they dry quickly after rain. It's also easy to get lost and, well, to hide. I had the presentiment we were being watched almost the whole time we were there."

"When Amalea told me that," Brad interrupted, "I called everyone together and said: 'Look. Rose made many enemies in the last year. She shouldn't be left alone. None of us should. Let's stick together as much as possible.'"

"And we followed that suggestion, though Rose sometimes would try the hardest grade climbs with Jason and Will," Amalea continued. Jason and Will, both slim but extremely strong, approached us. Back in White Salmon, Washington, Jason had started a guide service for the best of the best — he would take them to unnamed cliffs and they would warm up on 5.13A routes and go up from there. Will wrote screenplays between climbing trips.

"The climbing here is different from what we know," Jason said. "We are cliff climbers when we're at the Columbia Gorge and Smith Rock. Fontainebleau offers tiny finger holds, sometimes fingernail holds, but a great surface. We just came to have fun. And now this."

"One day an old man, leaning on a cane, came round to watch the three of us," Will said. "We were near Elephant Rock at Larchant. The surface is sand, but the boulders are high, so the climbs require a lot of focus. The man stood there and watched Jason and me, but even more so, Rose."

"I don't like it when people watch me," Jason added. "Unless I know them. But this guy felt familiar. So I asked him who he was.

"'Christien de la Foi,' he replied. 'I put up all the blue routes and most of the green/black ones here. Once a friend and I did all of the orange routes in 40 minutes. It takes some people three days.'"

"It was a famous name," Jason went on, "but I wasn't sure, so I asked him for some beta for a route I was trying. 'Pull up. Throw yourself at an angle of 70 degrees to the left, rotate the right hand to a mantle, and you are up,' the old guy said. He was spot on. We kept climbing and he kept watching. Finally we stopped for a cigarette."

"By this time, we all had come over," Amalea said. "The old man didn't want to shake hands, but he looked us over. 'These three,' he said, indicating Will, Jason, and Rose, 'are not bad. Americans are usually troublemakers when it comes to climbing, but these are okay. We have a philosophy here at Elephant Rock: Only idiots fall. You three are not idiots.'"

"A big compliment from a Frenchman, I suppose," Jason interrupted with a chuckle.

Will continued the story. "Then the guy leaned his cane against a rock and pulled out what looked like a scroll. He turned to Rose and said, 'Please read this.'"

"'No, we're just here to climb,'" Rose responded, turning away to walk to the next boulder.

"'It's a poem,' the old man said. 'Please.'"

"We kept the scroll," Will said, as he handed it to Ecco, who read it aloud: "From far in the west, strong and shining red, she will come to us. She will know our riddles and our songs."

Will continued his narrative. "'C'est vous, mademoiselle,' the man said, addressing Rose, whose bright red hair was collected together in a headband. 'You have already passed the first test — strong and shining red.'

"'What's all this about?' Rose asked.

"'I am a Templar,' said the old man. 'You know us. More properly, you know our fallen children. The so-called Warriors of the Rapture, the leaders anyway, descend from a long line of Templars. Please come back to Paris with us, all of you. We need your help with some messages we've found. '"

Scot interrupted Will: "I told the guy, 'Look, man, we came to climb. The only thing we know about Paris is that the Eiffel Tower is there, but it's off limits to climbers and the outside skin looks too easy to climb anyway. Also, just because we're Americans doesn't mean we think every Frenchman stepped out of the *Da Vinci Code*. '"

"'Ah yes, but we need you,' said the old guy. 'Quite desperately. If it's money you want, we can give you gold coins, Byzantine gold coins from our secret treasury. We need you only for three days. We have a beautiful apartment in the center of Paris which you'll find very comfortable, I assure you.'"

Cheri came next to Scot and put her arm on his shoulder to calm him. Smiling sheepishly, she said, "Okay, look, I'm always thinking of ways of paying off my student loans. Gold coins sounded like a cool way to do it. So, I argued for this: 'In my medieval art history course, the prof talked a lot about the Templars. They were crazy wealthy. Let's give this a chance. We'll be together. Also, I could use a real shower. '"

Brad took over the narrative. "I don't know why. But this convinced us. We did need a rest and figured a paid stay in Paris couldn't be that bad. Also, we'd all be together, so what could they do? So, we came back three days ago. They put us up in an apartment on the Left Bank overlooking the Seine and the Louvre. They let us rest the first day and they sent up amazing food from Fauchon.

"The second day, in the afternoon, the old guy came with two other men all about the same age, late 60s I would say.

"'We've brought your coins,'" the old guy with the cane said. 'Wealth won't bring you happiness, but your youth prevents you from knowing that.'" His two assistants handed out bags filled with clean but obviously old gold coins, each one having the double cross of the Byzantine church. 'We trust you and we need you — tonight.' He explained that we were to copy down messages from plaques in various parts of Paris. "'We will take each of you to a different place. We need you to copy down exactly what you see. We will blindfold you because our routes there and back will be, well, unusual,' the old guy explained."

"We had no idea why they needed us to do this, but the coins seemed to quiet all debate," Brad went on, "especially after Cheri went to a coin dealer in the Marais and confirmed that they were real."

"Interesting," said Ecco. "At least you weren't scammed. That's quite surprising, even worrisome because it means they are clearly serious people. I wonder what Rose knows that they need to find out."

"Only Will and Jason didn't want anything more to do with this," Brad replied.

"Yeah," said Will. "I wondered why they couldn't copy the inscriptions themselves. Also, I didn't care about the money. I came here to climb. But I guess we were seduced by the adventure of it all."

"Around midnight last night," Amalea continued. "We were blindfolded and taken out, each of us to a different place. Sometimes we were taken down tunnels. It took almost four hours for each of us. We were each asked to copy an inscription, and then we were blindfolded again and led back to the fountain at Place St. Sulpice. When we went back to the flat the Templars had given us, Rose was gone. We called Kate. We've been looking for Rose all day. Pete, Christie, and Mike are still looking."

"I don't think you'll find her enjoying the sights," Ecco said. "Let's take a look at these inscriptions and wait for the others to arrive. I'd like to ask each of you to tell me what you remember about the place you were taken to."

Cheri spoke first. "There was a tall greenish column on an elaborate stand, though I was led down a nearby side street. Here is the inscription I copied." She handed Ecco a piece of lined paper on which she had copied the encrypted message:

Zyl Adu Ao oKu zJAGu bu JA mAToqJJu. LlTo AT wyl TKylJbW'o nJAYu VGyo yd RKudq, wyl WuubW'o cyddw Anylo NyTu. Iu YuAW Kud Wy KAdY. Iu jlTo Wuub qWsydYAoqyW. IKw GylJbW'o cu jlTo ATi Kud? IuJJ, qW Kud GyWTGqylT YqWb, TKu YAw Wyo duYuYnud, nlo Kud lWGyWTqylT YAw. Iu YlTo Odynu qo.

Will was next. "There was a tramway and I saw a cafe called *Rond* something. A pretty major intersection."

bUi rFV rd oUFdV K'BFxVrsj. MUF VQrTGxV, DV dUUC UHVF dwV zrdwj rd gxisJ, FrdwVF XrF XFUT DwVFV JUi rFV sUD. kwUjV wrK DUsKVFXix dissVxj. tV rxjU TrsrAVK dwV VrFxIVjd LrdrLUTzj—ziFJIsA jCVxVdUsj rsK dFVrjiFV DwVs DV xVrFsVK UX dwV rddrLC zJ owIxIGGV Za.

Then Jason. "They took me around in circles. Finally, I arrived near the back of a large church. There were gargoyles everywhere."

jzn huJ hv yzvuJ WhYJ. OhR UJ lnuH oH UJTT, vUhv JtoT cUoToffJ Mk. xJ UhV XuzFH rJhTznC zS znu FJhTvU hHV UhV YzCv zS nC YnuVJuJV—lnuHJV hv vUJ Cvhmj. Mv'C h TJCCzH zS UoCvzuR vUhv oS hH oVJHvoSohlTJ Xuznf FovUznv CnlCvhHvohT vUuJhv zS SzuKJ lJKzYJC vzz FJhTvuR, ovC FJhTvU FoTT lJ CvzTJH. Mv FhC hC vunJ Szu nC oH vUzCJ RJhuC zS SouJ hC ov UhC lJJH Szu vUJ IUoHJCJ zS CznvUJhCv LCoh. bJ FJuJ fhuvTR hv ShnTv.

"Could be any of the grand churches of Paris," said Ecco.

Scot went next. "I saw a large sculpture with many figures and a woman taking a step forward with her right hand out."

FP1 wvk wp CIwNk bk Iw xwphPO. Hk yIwlOpkb Plv ukwIpX pPP LlNX. TXPljX Plv Pvbkv Xwb Wpwvpkb wW POk Py qPPv ZOhjXpW, uk Xwb wNKlhvkb IwObW wOb LkwOW Py LwOlywNplvk wOb, pXvPljX Plv WkvYhNkW pP qhIjvhLW, YwWp LPOkpwvQ ukwIpX. Hk ukvk IPPZkb PO uhpX WlWqhNhPO wOb nkwIPlWQ. TuP NkOplvhkW wypkv Plv Okwv pPpwI bkWpvlNphPO, SwvphO flpXkv Nvkwpkb wO wIpkvOwpk AXvhWphwO YhWhPO.

"You all were lucky," said Amalea. "They took me to a noisy train station."

SxT aYn aV Vjn CaYn Gn qJxt. SxT WnYn ETPVn QTIIPMIn. 1FnYPNatO xsVnt NjaOn asVnY QYnaV WnaIVj. mTV GYnaFO xs YPNjnO VnFvV FatJ vnxvIn, Ox JxT aYn txV aIxtn. CxIG atG OVxYPnO xs atNPntV NxPtO FaXn vnxvIn IxOn aII YnaOxt. 1V Vjn jnPQjVjV xs xTY vxWnY Pt Vjn IaVn 13Vj NntVTYJ, Wn FatPvTIaVnG vaTvnYO atG vYPtNnO WPvj jatGsTIO xs QxIG. wxt'V MIaFn DjnYP atG UNxV. UNxV WaO MaGIJ YxTQjnG Tv MJ VjxOn jnaVjnt baYYPxYO xs Vjn havVYn. in tnnGnG a ITNXJ MYnaX. DjnYP tnnGnG Vjn FxtnJ. Zjn NxPtO aYn YnaI. Ujn'II Mn aMIn Vx vaJ xss jnY NYnGPVxYO. Zxx MaG TtPPnYOPVPnO Pt 1FnYPNa aYn Ox ngvntOPpn.

Part III: Faithful Foes

By this time, Pete, Christie, and Mike had returned. Their faces showed that they hadn't found Rose. Cheri explained to them Ecco's current theory that Rose was probably kidnapped but unharmed.

Brad spoke up next. "All I can tell you is that my inscription was on the side of a door at an Irish bar," he said. "There was a sculpture of a woman in armor on a horse at an intersection nearby."

FUO MnX Mh hiX CeMYX mXMggX R'wnY. FUO xMS gUh ZgUo hisk, POh CMnsk, PXeUo
hiX pnUOgR, nXkXxPeXk M eMnpX koskk YiXXkX. tinUOpi hiX eUgp iskhUnS UT
hiX YshS, XjXg oiXg hiX YshS oMk YMeeXR EOhXzsM PS hiX vUxMgk, CMnsksMgk
ROp hOggXek OgRXnpnUOgR hU pXh POseRsgp xMhXnsMe. bg 17hi MgR 18hi
YXghOnsXk, Xghsnx khnXXhk UT CMnsk YUeeMakXR PXYMOkX UT hiX koskk
YiXXkX-esZX YMjXngk OgRXngXMhi (oX cnXgYi YMee hisk pnOSXnX). bg 1777,
GOseeMOxUh, kXYnXheS UT UOn UnRXn, oMk MaaUsghXR hU hMZX YiMnpX UT hiX
OgRXnpnUOgR aMkkMpXoMSk sg UnRXn hU anXjXgh hiXx TnUx YUeeMaksgp. BX
YeUkXR UTT kUxX hOggXek, nXsgTUnYXR UhiXnk TUn aOPesY OkX, MgR ZXah M TXo
TUn UOn ansjMhX OkX. dUxX UT hiX PXkh MnX hiX UeRXkh, XkaXYsMeeS sg oiMh
sk gUo hiX TsThi MnnUgRskXxXgh.

"Figures you'd notice what you can drink," said Amalea with a friendly chuckle. How could she sound so relaxed? Was she convinced by Ecco that Rose was okay? I wasn't.

"I'll go next," said Mike. "I went to a building near a garden with a large pond in a basin."

RsY ILa IQ Da faqIQ. fsna sv sYL qYnbaL, ts vYLVsYt IQ Qja GjYLGj sv hsna
vsL VQt HILQVGVHIQVsq Vq sYL qaIL aKQaLnVqIQVsq, gsVqaZ VQ. Ja jINa
IodIpt HLsNVZaZ Qja GjVoZLaq sv DYQjaL dVQj QjaVL nstQ ZaZVGIQaZ
nanbaLt. SqvsLQYqIQaop, tsna QYLq Qs vIqIQVVGVtn—atHaGVIoop LaiILZVqi
Qja nVtYqZaLtssZ bssM sv haNaoIQVsq. CjIQ Vt djaLa Qja JILLVsLt sv Qja
hIHQYLa Gsna Vq. Ja QjVqM Qjap jIZ HoIqqaZ bVi QjVqit, bVi, bIZ, IqZ
ZatQLYGQVNa. CjaVL tYGGattsLt GIoo QjantaoNat cIoo sv kIbposq. Cjap ILa
nsLa vIqIQVGVIo tQVoo. Oj, da IiLaa Qja dsLoZ jIt baGsna bIZ. kaIYQp, MVZt
HoIpVqi IqZ oIYijQaL dIqQ Qs ba YqVNaLtIo. mqtQaIZ da jINa HsdaL nIZqatt,
iLaaZ, ZVLQp bsnbt, GoYtQaL bsnbt IqZ jIVLtHLIp bsnbt. kYQ Qjap Zsq'Q
dIqQ HaIGa. JjIQ Qjap dIqQ Vt I GoaIqtVqi dIL, djIQaNaL QjIQ nVijQ naIq.

"Was it close by?" asked Ecco.

"Could have been," answered Mike. "They took me around in circles."

"I was at a train station, lots of homeless guys sleeping just outside," said Christie.

mRx bNv bf fKv HbNv B'axufvNzYfP. 1KvF jv ubI jv bNv QRYFQ fR GNRpv KvN
xFCRFuCYRxu TYFB, jv BYB FRf TvbF fKYu YF b pbB jbI. 1v BRF'f xuv BNxQu.
AxN RNBvN JFRju TbFI uvCNvf bFB GbYFzvuu jbIu RX bCZxYNYFQ YFXRNTbfYRF
XNRT GvRGzv. 1v xuvB KIGFRuYu jbI pvXRNv yvuTvN. 1v pNRxQKf Yf pbCJ XNRT
RxN wYuYfu fR gRGfYC qQIGf. DRuv jYzz pv ubXv XNRT bzz BYufNbCfYRF YF RxN
fxFFvzu pvFvbfK hbNYu.

"Maybe it's the same one I was at," Amalea said.

"Could be," said Ecco, "but I don't think so. I don't think they would have wanted you to communicate."

"But I was also at a train station" said Pete. He was muscular and he smiled, but he looked vaguely frightening in his dreadlocks. Rose had told us during our flight to France that she had just met him. He had asked to come along when he heard she was planning a climbing trip. "My train station had lots of glass and lots of escalators, mostly above ground. The neighborhood outside had lots of lights, lots of pretty girls, lots of action."

 jkr BuY BM MHY LBuY mY QksMSBusBZZY. ek ZMBuM, qY HBTY Bs BSkckpt Mk zBCY.
AY eYzScBuZ BuY ls JBbM Bs HkskuBncY lJ ZYbuYMlTY ZkblYMt. UrM Hksku
mkYZs'M SuYbcrmY kbbBZlksBc mYbYSMlks. aTYs UYusBum mY XcBluTBrK HBm Mk
SukzlZY zkuY MHBs qY HBm Mk kJJYu ls kru YBuclYZM tYBuZ. Dk lM lZ MHBM qY
HBTY mYbYlTYm tkr ls kumYu Mk ZYSBuBMY tkr Jukz OkZY. AY HBTY nYsM tkru
YBuZ qlMH muYBzZ kJ ulbHYZ Bsm tkr BcckqYm tkruZYcTYZ Mk nY SYuZrBmYm.

Ecco laid all the inscriptions and Rose's letter in front of him. "Our first objective is to crack the codes and hope they lead us to Rose," Ecco said. "I wonder what role the Sudoku plays in all this."

He paused in silence. "While I work on the codes, Jason, please visit all major churches and see if you find something familiar. Pete, Christie, and Amalea, do the same with the train stations. You three stay together. Will, please go with Jason. I don't want any more disappearances. Brad, you can stay here. In all of French history, which woman is likely to be riding a horse in armor? In fact, let's start with your letter."

Turning to me, he said, "Professor, would you be so kind as to give me some computer help?"

I nodded and Ecco set to work. A few hours later, we had worked out all the inscriptions. My programs helped try possible codes. The first we cracked was Brad's:

You are at the Place Jeanne d'Arc. You may not know this, but Paris, below the ground, resembles a large swiss cheese. Through the long history of the city, even when the city was called Lutezia by the Romans, Parisians dug tunnels underground to get building material. In 17th and 18th centuries, entire streets of Paris collapsed because of the swiss cheese–like caverns underneath (we French call this gruyere). In 1777, Guillaumot, secretly of our order, was appointed to take charge of the underground passageways in order to prevent them from collapsing. He closed off some tunnels, reinforced others for public use, and kept a few for our private use. Some of the best are the oldest, especially in what is now the fifth arrondisement.

Next we worked on Rose's letter. It took until the next morning to find the correct solution to the Sudoku, as there were several possibilities. My help wasn't so useful for that until the end.

"Tunnels. Of course," said Ecco after studying the map. "I know where to go."

 Puzzle Contestant: *Please send in translations of all the inscriptions, Rose's letter, and a good solution to the Sudoku. Find the theatre close to the balance point. (You'll know what that means after you decrypt Rose's letter.)*

We found the theatre. There were several possible tunnel entrances. Ecco began to check out each one systematically. At the third one, he descended a few steps, then looked up at us and said, "Do you want to hear the good news first or the bad?"

"The good," we replied in unison.

"This is the correct entrance," he replied.

"And the bad?" we asked.

"There is another encrypted message to decipher," he said. "Professor, are you available?" He pointed out a message on a small plaque:

GbzLVyb, tg. hLLV. jVg fu yxpu Sb IVx fO IVx'sb LVyb umfp OBg. qVx'zz Sb
BSzb uV OfCv xp. Hxu vVC'u Qbu zVpu. Gb, fCLzxvfCQ DVpb, Bgb XfumfC 160
ybubgp VO umfp bCugBCLb, Sxu fu'p sbgI vBgK. Umb uxCCbzp Bgb Bzz Bu B
pfCQzb zbsbz, Sxu Xb yBI Sb fC BC fCubgfVg gVVy. GmbC IVx OfCv xp, IVx'zz
KCVX fu SbLBxpb umb puVCb fp gbAzBLbv SI pyVVum pubbz.

"Scot, you brought rope with you to France, didn't you?" Ecco asked.

"Yes, two 60 meter ropes and one 40," Scot replied. "We were thinking of going cliff climbing in Bourgogne."

"Please bring all three ropes and some webbing to link them. Pete, please go with him," Ecco said. "Cheri, your French is the best. Please take Will and Jason and get us five or six flashlights with plenty of batteries."

When Scot and Pete returned, Ecco asked them to attach the two ropes with the webbing. "Will and Jason, we'll wait for you here," Ecco said, handing them the flashlights Cheri had brought. "Inside, turn to the left every time you come to a fork in the tunnel. You are looking for a steel door. When you find it, leave the rope there and bring us all in. While you're looking, you may reach the end of the rope or a dead end. If so, back up to..."

A soccer ball had just hit Ecco on his head. The boy who kicked it came over. "*Excusez-moi Monsieur*," he said as he picked up the ball and ran away.

As Ecco was slightly dazed, I finished the instructions to Will and Jason.

 Puzzle Contestant: *Decrypt this final inscription, and finish the instructions as the professor might have.*

About an hour later, Will and Jason emerged. "We found it," they said.

In the meantime, Ecco had recovered from his soccer injury. We entered the tunnels. When we arrived at the steel door, an elderly man opened it before we knocked. Behind him stood Rose and behind her, with his back to us, sat a man in his forties.

Kate rushed in to embrace Rose, who looked slightly flushed but otherwise fine. "It's our spiked apple cider," said the old man who opened the door, now quite fine without the cane. "Combined with our secret techniques of hypnosis (Mesmer learned from us), it helped Rose remember exactly what she saw on the bridge. Dr. Ecco, I'm pleased to meet you. My name is Christien de la Foi. My apologies to you all. We needed this little time alone with Rose. She told us much valuable information concerning the precise description of the men who followed her in Ohio and the men who tried to corner her on the Hood River bridge in Oregon the fateful night of her dive into the Columbia. From her description, we are certain of who pursued her.

"Unfortunately, their identities make us worry even more. Calvert Warren is a fanatic. He is convinced he works for a holy cause and will kill without hesitation. His brother Elder is a forger. He will take on the identity of anyone who is 'not of the elect' for all kinds of purposes — to steal from them, to ruin their reputation, even to frame them. We believe he has already been at work against one of us.

"I know this is terribly impolite, but before I go on, could we ask your young companions, including Rose and Kate, to keep watch at the entrance? What we're about to reveal must stay in the smallest possible circle. Also, we're not sure that child with the soccer ball was entirely innocent. Please tell your friends not to leave the tunnel or to make too much noise.

"How did you know about the soccer ball?" Kate asked.

"We are an old order in touch with modern technology," said de la Foi. "We have sensors all around the amphitheatre. But our order has always embraced technology. When I was young, they sent me to school to learn assembly language. I was the first programmer of our order to use string processing for the records of databases. We had to work with kilobytes of memory, so every bit counted. ASCII was much too expensive an encoding."

He then turned to me and said: "Professor Scarlet, we'd appreciate it if you stay as we discuss this problem with Dr. Ecco. We know that you work closely with Ecco and we think your computer expertise may be of great help."

After the climbers, Rose, and Kate left, the man in the seat rose and walked towards us. "Dr. Ecco, it is good to see you again," he said. "Surely you remember me."

"Elmer Nuth, how could I forget?" said Ecco. "It was your fifty thousand dollars that enabled me to get the ballots out of Oregon."

"Quite right," said Nuth. "And you destroyed, or thought you destroyed, the Warriors of the Rapture in the process. They were on the side of good, I thought. And you made them appear to be criminals. I cursed you for that."

"But now you've changed your mind?" asked Ecco.

"They are thieves," Nuth replied. "Worse, they are violent, horrifically so. Now that Rose has told us whom she saw, I think I know what they want to do."

"More election tampering?" Ecco said with a sigh.

"Let me tell you the whole story," Nuth replied. "I supported the Warriors of the Rapture to help win the 2004 election. I wanted our candidate to win. I saw no reason not to cheat in the elections. Others had done it before us, and computerized voting made it so easy. The Warriors infiltrated voting machine companies and voting commissions. I knew I could trust them to work for the cause. They were so disciplined that the fact that they cooperated to change the course of the election has never been revealed, not even now. What Rose uncovered was the tip of a very deep iceberg. Ohio still had punch-card ballots in places. The real ones had to be gotten rid of. Anyway, we won the election and I was ready to go on with my life.

"But the Warriors had just begun. They take the Biblical book of Revelations seriously and they want to bring about the Great Tribulation. Once they told me they wanted their followers to hold all ranking officer positions in one ballistic missile submarine. At first, I laughed. What could that do for anyone? But I began to read up on the operational rules for submarines in case of war. They must enjoy a certain autonomy in case they can't communicate with base. If all ranking officers agree, the submarine can fire missiles even without external control. What if a submarine sent missiles towards New York and Moscow and Beijing after warning the faithful? A tidy little apocalypse."

"Are they really that crazy?" I asked in horror.

"The Righteous will go to heaven and that's what they want," Nuth went on. "Goodness will rule over the earth. It sounds so good and nobody can prove it won't happen—their internal logic is too perfect."

"But how could they want to destroy the earth?" I asked in horror.

"They are convinced of their cause," de la Foi replied. "I understand them in a way. People fear change. The world changes. People seek the old certainties—the more fundamental, the more certain."

"They failed in their first attempt to control a submarine," Nuth continued. "And then they came under investigation after the election fraud case. Whereas investigators managed to get some of the small fry, the big fish got away and formed The End of Babylon, known to insiders as the Tribulants.

"I couldn't support this madness, so I began to disassociate myself from them. By that time, however, Elder knew how to forge my signature. Suspecting my failing loyalties, Calvert came to inform me that I was leaving my house and giving him the keys to my cars. Knowing what Calvert was capable of, I did so immediately and came here to Paris to visit my brother Templars.

"In the meantime, Elder has tested his ability to move small amounts of funds among my three accounts at Chase, Citi, and Commerce banks by writing checks from one to the other. He hasn't taken any money out yet according to Christien who has friends at the bank, but I expect he will soon. They plan to bribe key computer operators and lower-level bureaucrats to get all their officers to serve on the same submarine. Nobody would believe us if we told them about this plot, especially because we ourselves don't know which officers are Tribulants. We must stop them from using that money."

"So how can I help you?" Ecco asked.

"Well, I have $3 million in the three bank accounts Elder has access to," answered Nuth. "He can forge my signature, but I can also write my signature, of course. When I left the apartment, I took one check from each account. The rules of each bank are the usual: If I write a check for an amount less than or equal to the account balance, the payment will go through. Otherwise the check will bounce.

"We want to send the checks out today. I want to guarantee to recover as much money as possible, even if I'm very unlucky. For how large an amount can I write a check?" Nuth asked.

 Puzzle Contestant: *How much do you think the check amounts should be?*

"If that is all you know, then $1 million from each account," Ecco answered. "At least one account must have at least that much, because if all had less, then the total wouldn't add up to $3 million. If you wrote checks for more and every account had exactly $1 million, then you would get nothing."

"Would it help if I wrote the first check, and then waited to see if it cleared before writing the others?" Nuth asked.

"It might, but there is no guarantee," Ecco replied.

 Puzzle Contestant: *Explain Ecco's reply.*

"What if I knew that one account (but I don't know which one) has at least $600,000 more than another one?" Nuth continued. "Then how well could I guarantee to do?"

I didn't hear that response.

"But no, my dear Elmer," de la Foi continued. "We know more than that. We know that one account has exactly $600,000 more than another and, in addition, that the larger of the two has the most money and the smaller of the two has the least money," de la Foi said. "Dr. Ecco, can we guarantee to get more than half the $3 million in that case even if we send all checks simultaneously to the banks?"

"Yes, you can get this much," Ecco replied after a few minutes, showing a figure to de la Foi.

"And what if we wrote one check, saw whether it cleared or not, then wrote the second and saw whether it cleared, and then wrote the third?" Nuth asked.

"In that case, you can net nearly $2 million," Ecco replied scribbling a number on a sheet of paper. "Here is the exact number."

 Puzzle Contestant: *Answer the question when there is a known $600,000 or more difference between one account and the other. Then answer the question assuming the difference between the highest and lowest is exactly $600,000, but all checks are sent simultaneously without the benefit of feedback. Then try the feedback case.*

The discussion with de la Foi had taken some time. Ecco had answered the questions. I could see fatigue had started to take over. "Gentlemen, we hope we've helped you with your money matters," Ecco said standing up and turning towards the door. "We'll be going now to get some fresh air and would be obliged if you didn't kidnap any of us again."

De la Foi bowed. "We are much in your debt," he said. "You have done more than we could hope and have given direct evidence of your great talent. We thank you."

Ecco turned to leave, but he found the door to be locked. He turned to de la Foi, his eyes flashing in anger.

"Unfortunately, we must ask you for another service," de la Foi said.

"Haven't I done enough?" Ecco asked between clenched teeth.

"We'd like you to endorse these checks," de la Foi replied. "They will be made out to you to an account we've opened for you at the Zurich Geheimbank."

Ecco looked at me, shaking his head in disbelief.

"But I don't want your money," Ecco said. "I came to windsurf and to protect Rose and Kate, not to get rich. Besides, the money would make me a marked man. Elder would figure out I received the checks and he would come after me. Why would I want that?"

"You don't," de la Foi answered, "but you must see that we have no alternative. Elmer can't write the checks to himself because they can forge his signature. It's out of the question for me to be involved. The inner order of Templars must remain secret. Others can drink cocktails at the Cafe des Templiers and tell stories about the Square du Temple, but we few who tend the flame of the movement and who know its innermost secrets must stay out of the public eye."

"Find somebody else," said Ecco firmly, as he walked towards the door. "Make the money out to a herder in Mongolia if you have to. I'm in no need of the money and don't want to run this risk."

"That we cannot do," said de la Foi. "If we wrote the check to an innocent third party, Calvert would come to break his neck."

"And why won't he do the same to me?" asked Ecco.

"Because Elder will stop him," de la Foi replied. "Calvert always defers to Elder and Elder will not be able to resist trying to outsmart the great Dr. Ecco."

"Suppose I believe that," Ecco replied. "Suppose he tries to outsmart me and he fails. Then won't I have Calvert on my neck?"

"No," de la Foi replied. "We just need a little time to locate them. Within a few days of their contacting you, we'll be ready. *Ecoutez*, Dr. Ecco, we know we are asking you a lot. We are convinced that if you don't help us, millions will die. We implore you to accept."

Ecco sighed. "Professor," he turned to me. "Please tell Kate to fly back to the States, take the twins out of school, and to go on a long trip. She is to use cash everywhere. I will treat Rose and her climbing friends to a long tour of the Bourgogne. They won't be hard to convince."

Turning towards de la Foi, he said, "Okay, you win. It's all coming together to me now. You kidnapped Rose to get me to come find you. You knew I'd come to France, too. How could you know that? The Babylon Falls notes I found in my mailbox came from you, too, didn't they?"

"Not the first one, but the later ones," de la Foi admitted. "We need you, Ecco. The Tribulants are watching your apartment. We are watching them. For your safety and for ours and for the sake of humanity, we wanted you in France."

"I hope your cleverness lasts," Ecco said. "What next?"

"We have found a house for you in the south of France near Brive," de la Foi said. "It has only nine inhabitants now, but it was a thriving village in the 1500s. You will be safe there at least for a while. Strangers are easily noticed. Elder will propose a betting game. In spite of his religious ravings, he's an incorrigible gambler. You will demand that he use an escrow account. Once he does that, we'll be able to track him down and alert the authorities. He always uses the same escrow agent."

De la Foi looked at his watch. "It is dark outside, so I think we can gather your young friends and follow the tunnels to Cluny."

That evening, Ecco and I took the train to Brive, while Kate, Rose, and most of her friends headed off to Bourgogne. We were met at the station and taken to the tiny hamlet of St. Pal. Pete, Mike, and Christie came with us. "A little extra protection has got to be good, doc," Pete said. It occurred to me that we didn't really know these climbers, especially Pete, the newest addition to Rose's circle of friends. Should we trust them?

"I agree, Professor, it's a risk," Ecco said to me. "But if they're bad, I'd rather that they be far from Rose."

We settled into a sixteenth century stone manor house with a conical tower. For the Templars, towers played the role of lookout and treasury, but the door up to this tower was locked. The house was comfortably appointed and the stone walls made it cool but never cold. A few steps away, there was a Roman bath, also lined with stone, that children used in the summer. In the other direction stood a large and well-maintained church, a sign of the thriving agricultural community that was once centered on the market at St. Pal. Ecco remained inside the house or sat in the garden for a few days. The garden had a thick wall of prickly rose bushes everywhere except for a small gap leading to a neighboring field. Ecco avoided that gap.

"There is nothing to do until the checks clear," he explained as he lounged in the garden reading a textbook about Swiss banking laws.

The third day after our arrival, we received a phone call. "Geheimbank has your money," de la Foi told Ecco. "In the wine cellar, behind the Burgundy, you'll find the bank codes."

Ecco checked his account. "Nearly $2 million," he said. "It's bait and so are we. Let's see where they bite."

Part III: Faithful Foes

Finally, an email arrived:

> Dr. Ecco,
>
> The first round goes to you. But we still have more to go. Everyone says you are smart, but the check writing was sheer luck.
>
> In the meantime, I need the money back for my projects. I propose a bet on a game based on Nim. The basic Nim game goes like this. Start with 20 sticks. Each player may take one, two, or three sticks per turn until there are none left. The last player to remove a stick loses.
>
> If I'm the first player, there is a winning strategy, as someone of your great intelligence must know: Work backwards from the end. I know that I win, if I leave you just one stick. That means that if I leave you five sticks, then I will win because no matter how many you take, I can end up leaving you one. For example, if you take two, I will take two. If you take three, I will take one. Similarly if I leave you nine sticks, I can guarantee to leave you five sticks the next time you go. That will ensure a win for me. Starting at one, and increasing by four each time, we get 5, 9, 13, and 17. Therefore, in my first move, I take away three, leaving you with 17, and thereby ensuring my victory.
>
> I have several variants, which I would like us to bet about. In every variant, I will go first, but I will give you a choice of the number of sticks we begin with between 20 and 25 inclusive. We will then play for an even money bet. Do you agree to these conditions?
>
> May the Righteous Prevail,
>
> Elder

Dr. Ecco turned to me. "So far, de la Foi is right about the money and the contact," he said. "But this guy is way too confident—'great intelligence' indeed."

Ecco didn't answer Elder for several hours. A new email appeared, a lot less friendly.

> Dear Dr. Ecco,
>
> Calvert has located you to near Brive. We also know that your bank is the Geheimbank of Zurich. I hope you agree to play.
>
> May the Righteous Prevail,
>
> Elder

"How could Calvert be so close?" I asked, horrified at the thought of this muscular ex-Marine strangling us in our sleep. "Who knew we were here? The climbers, Kate, and the Templars. Whom can we trust?"

"I think the climbers are trustworthy," Ecco replied. "In any case, I think we have to try this bet and hope the escrow account trap works."

> Dear Elder,
>
> Please call me Jake. I would love to play with you. If we play for money, we both want to be sure the other will pay up if he loses. So once we agree on a wager, we should both pay into an escrow account.
>
> All the best,
>
> Jake

After sending the email, Ecco motioned to me to go to the garden. Under a tree and in a low voice he said: "We've got to figure out who told Elder our whereabouts. Of the people we have met, only Nuth and de la Foi know which bank I used. I don't think they're suspects.

"De la Foi could easily have taken the money for himself from the beginning. Anyway, the fact that he gave real gold coins to the kids suggests he is in no need of cash. Likewise, why would Nuth use up his checks if he wanted the Tribulants to end up with it in the end? It's possible that there is a Tribulant among the climbers here with us, but if all three or even two were Tribulants they could have compelled me by force by now. Also, de la Foi never told them about Geheimbank. I guess it's possible that one of them is a Tribulant and is just biding his time. But my intuitions are against this.

"I think it's more likely that the Templars have a spy in their midst. Didn't de la Foi tell us the Warriors were fallen Templars? He also mentioned that the Templars were an old order conversant in high technology. Suppose someone were eavesdropping on our conversation with Nuth and de la Foi. Such a person would not have the bank account information, but might have at least an idea where we were, though not precisely, because de la Foi didn't say so out loud.

"Should we encrypt a letter to de la Foi?" I asked.

"How to do it—that's the question," Ecco replied. "If another Templar is a spy, he may know the style of code de la Foi used in the inscriptions. We must give de la Foi a message that he is uniquely likely to decrypt even though it will be short."

Part III: Faithful Foes

Ecco went to his desk. Fifteen minutes later he came out with:

101752467A44B405C4801E3409E8314549AB1DDA22E44D29AEB42

"Hexadecimal, isn't it?" I asked.

 Puzzle Contestant: You should decrypt this one.

"Indeed Professor," Ecco replied. "Please send it to de la Foi. I'll explain the code to you later."

Elder's next email had already arrived.

> Jake, Jake the red-haired snake.
>
> I know that old de la Foi has prepared to trap me with the escrow. He thinks I'm going to use Idaho Trust. But I think they've been infiltrated by Feds and other riff-raff. So we'll use Sheila's Trust Bank on the Isle of Man instead.
>
> Here are the rules of our first game. Call it Exclusion Nim. The rules of Nim remain the same except that a player may not remove the same number of sticks as the previous player unless only one stick remains and the previous player removed one stick. For example, if player A takes two sticks, the other player may take one or three but not two sticks in the turn following. I go first, so I have no constraint in my first move, but you may demand that we start with any number of sticks between 20 and 25 inclusive.
>
> I challenge you to a $100,000 wager. If you agree, propose a number of sticks and deposit that amount with Sheila.
>
> Righteous,
>
> Elder

Ecco looked at me puzzled. "Why would he throw away his money like this?" he asked shaking his head. "Anyway, I will send another message to de la Foi. Encrypt it using the same encoding I used in my last message to him: 'elder wants to use sheila trust in the isle of man"

 Puzzle Contestant: You should encrypt this one.

> **Dear Elder,**
>
> **I accept. Please start with 21 sticks. My money is in the Isle of Man.**
>
> **Warmest Regards,**
>
> **Jake**

The game was an easy win for Ecco.

```
Pile starts with 21
Elder removes 3
Ecco: 1
Elder: 1
Ecco: 3
Elder: 2
Ecco: 1
Elder: 3
Ecco: 2
Elder: 3
Ecco: 1
Elder: 1
```

A new email arrived soon afterwards:

> You are not bad, Ecco.
>
> This time, I go first and I start with 20 sticks. We still play Exclusion Nim except you have one advantage. You can choose some number about which you can't be excluded—called an exclusion exception. For example, suppose you choose the 3 as an exclusion exception. Then, even if I remove three sticks, you may remove three in the next turn. In that case, however, if I remove one stick, you may not remove one next and similarly for two.
>
> This time I propose a bet of $200,000—double or nothing.
>
> Elder

"I think he's getting upset," I told Ecco.

"How do you know?" Ecco asked.

"No more 'Righteous,'" I replied. We both laughed.

"I still don't understand why he's proposing games that he is sure to lose," Ecco said. "Maybe he wants me to stay in one place while Calvert comes in for the kill? Let's call in the climbers."

We went outside and found Mike scaling the bell tower of the church. Christie was belaying from the ground and Pete was yelling advice.

"After you reach the top, would you mind coming down, Mike?" Ecco said from below. "I need to talk to all three of you in the garden."

"Sure, doc," Mike said. Straddling the corner of the tower, heels down and hands and feet hugging the tiny cracks, he made it to the belfry. A minute later, all three were under the tree Ecco had reserved for important conversations. I began to realize he thought the house might be bugged.

"As you've guessed," Ecco began, "we've been put here to stay out of harm's way."

They all nodded.

"Well, harm is following us. You have to know that the man who is coming after us is merciless, strong, and fanatical. He may have equally unsavory friends with him. He wants money from a bank account and he'll do whatever he has to do to get it from me. If any of you want to join Rose at the Bourgogne, now is the time."

"No way," said Pete to the nodded agreement of the others. "That's why we're here. Our job is to keep harm away. We've been laying traps around the house. Nothing electronic. Just clear plastic cables that will tug a bell here or there if someone crosses the gap between the hedges. I think that's the natural avenue of attack. We don't know what they'll come in with, so we think it's better to hide rather than fight. If we're attacked, one of us will distract the intruders while others wake you up and take you by underground passage to the church. We've found a room for you just below the belfry. The bells will ring every hour after 7 A.M. every morning, but you'll be safe, as long as you need to hide there."

Ecco nodded his head in admiration. "How did you know to do all this?" he asked of Pete. "Did you grow your dreadlocks after serving in the special forces?"

"I just see a lot of movies," said Pete. It was one of those boastfully modest denials in the spirit of 'I'm just a country lawyer.'

"I guess that means I'll be sleeping on the couch downstairs for a few days," said Ecco.

"Right," said Mike. "One of us will be on the lookout every night."

"I'll also stay awake from 4 A.M. on," I volunteered.

"Great, so I'll have two guardian angels," Ecco replied with a smile. "There's something else I want to see, but we'll have to go inside for that."

We followed him inside and he invited us all to sit down. Ecco picked up a simple wooden cross and began twirling it in his hands as if to gauge our reactions. He smiled at us as he did this. I remember thinking how strange this was because Ecco had never before shown any interest in religious objects.

Suddenly, he hurled the cross across the room at the mantle just below the fireplace.

Pete leapt to his feet. "Burn in hell!" he yelled as he rushed towards Ecco. Ecco prepared to defend himself but then Pete just stopped, placing a hand on a table as if to steady himself. He then slumped into the nearest chair, put his head in his hands, and began to sob. Ecco put his hand on his shoulder. "Talk to us, Pete," he said gently. "Tell us where you're from, what you believe in."

"They took me out of my misery," Pete said slowly. "Drugs, alcohol, anything that could let me sleep through the night after all the death I had seen in missions that never hit the newspapers. They promised me peace and salvation. They cared for me, or so I thought. I learned the Bible. We read Revelations over and over. Then one day they changed their tune. They kept repeating that world peace required a great outpouring of blood. They called themselves the Warriors. Knowing my military background as a Navy SEAL, they asked me to train them. They talked about death as cleansing. One day they talked to me about a 'witch' named Rose who had done the Warriors a bad deed. They showed me a picture. The clear eyes, the beautiful features — she looked more like an avenging angel to me.

"A week later, a late July day, I just left. It was easy to find cover in the trees where we were training and I made my way to Portland. Then up to Hood River. I slept among the vans that the windsurfers used as mobile homes in the Walmart parking lot and I hooked up with some climbers. Finally, I met Rose, even stronger and more beautiful than in the picture. I knew the Warriors would want revenge. She needed protection. So I joined her group of friends. I didn't tell them what I knew; they just thought of me as a fellow climber.

"You've got to believe me. I don't want to hurt you and I certainly don't want to hurt Rose. But I must ask you. No more throwing crosses. I know why you did it, but please don't do it again."

"Yes, I do believe you," said Ecco. "If you had been still on their side, you could have taken out Christie and caused Mike to fall to his death. Still, I had to know your real story."

Mike, Christie, and I slowly recovered from what we had seen and heard. Finally, Christie asked, "If the gap is the place where they'll come, why don't we block it?"

"Got to give them a place to attack," Pete said. "I'm going to plant some surprises for them if they come that way. Avoid that part of the grounds."

The three of them went outside and Ecco returned to his email. "Well, Professor, what do you think?" he asked. "Should I choose an exemption that will guarantee me a win or that will allow Elder to win?"

"Let him win," I suggested. "We need him to underestimate us. Also, maybe he'll call off Calvert."

"My thought exactly," Ecco said. "I'll make my exclusion exemption be 2."

The game proceeded by email exchange:

```
Pile starts with 20:
Elder removes 3
Ecco: 3
Elder: 1
Ecco: 2
Elder: 1
Ecco: 2
Elder: 3
Ecco: 1
Elder: 3
Ecco: 1
```

Then came the email:

> To the <u>great</u> Dr. Ecco:
>
> And I thought you were so good at games. You, too, have feet of clay!
>
> The Righteous Prevail,
>
> Elder

 Puzzle Contestant*: Could Ecco have chosen a different exclusion exemption and have guaranteed to win? If so, state which one and prove that you have a winning strategy. If not, show that Elder has a winning strategy when he goes first with 20 sticks no matter what.*

Ecco chuckled. "Let him have his fun," he said. "Every day that passes is a day that he doesn't have his money.... He's clever though. Not only did he switch escrow accounts to avoid being caught himself, but I wouldn't be surprised if he had some way of getting my signature from Sheila."

It took less than a day for us to receive our next message.

> Ecco,
>
> No more fun and games. I know you have eight accounts at Geheimbank. Very prudent of you to spread your eggs in more baskets than I used. Fortunately for me, I have a check for each account. Oh yes, we have sympathizers all over.
>
> I also know their rules: If even one check bounces on any account, then all accounts will be frozen from the end of business on that day until you appear in person to get your money.

Why am I telling you all this? First, to tell you that you'll have to move to get your money. But second, to tell you that there won't be much left. My eight checks will all be for the same amount and I expect to get at least a million from your accounts before the bank freezes them. It's up to you to figure out the amount.

The Righteous Prevail,

Elder

"I see our loss resuscitated his arrogance," Ecco said, shaking his head. "He didn't like the fact that I got well more than half his money when Elmer wrote the checks. The question is whether I can prevent him from getting more than half of what I have left. What do you think, Professor?"

"It will be a difficult psychological task to figure out the amount he's going to write," I said. "He could choose a large amount in the hope that you'll concentrate your funds in a few large accounts. Or he could choose a small amount, 1/8 of your total in case you distribute evenly."

"Penetrating the psychology of a criminal mind is not my method, Professor, you know that," Ecco said. "Let's look at the problem mathematically. We want to distribute the amounts in the accounts so that no matter which amount he writes, he will get half or less of what I have there. Given that he's already won $100,000 from me through my loss at Nim, it would seem that he's on a roll."

Ecco paused a moment. "One non-mathematical tactic we have at our disposal is to write large checks ourselves," he said. "If ours arrives first, his will all bounce."

Ecco wrote a check for $3 million and gave it to me. "Please go to town and send this by Chronopost," he said. "In the meantime, I'll move around the amounts in the accounts in case his checks arrive first."

 Puzzle Contestant: *All Ecco can do is to shift funds from one account to the other. How should he do that in order to prevent Elder from getting more than half of what Ecco has in Geheimbank, no matter which amount Elder chooses to write on all the checks? The rules are as before: A check that is less than or equal to the amount in an account will be honored. If more, then the check will bounce.*

By the time I came back, Ecco sat on the couch, now most of the way through the Swiss banking law book. "What now?" I asked.

"When an animal is angry, it acts decisively and impulsively," Ecco responded. "Elder, behind those godly pretensions, will rediscover his animal nature when he finds that he gets less than 45 percent of the money at most. The question is: How will he act? My hope is he doesn't understand the Swiss as well as I do."

With that, he showed me his message to de la Foi:

091682549A22C648EAC85AF4676A6ED6691408FA9BB410355A09351200780

 Puzzle Contestant: *Decipher the message.*

As Ecco predicted, Elder flew to Zurich traveling under the name Jacob Ecco. The Swiss police arrested him as he presented his forged papers to the bank officer. The French police caught Calvert when he attacked an undercover agent in Brive whose orange hair and lanky frame made him resemble Dr. Ecco. De la Foi had tipped off the police, but had given no background information.

"I didn't need to," de la Foi explained at the banquet prepared in our honor at a discrete chateau in Rambouillet a week later. "The Swiss throw you in prison if you can't pay your debts. They punish banking fraud with far more severity. As for the French, the police really don't like their brother police officers to be attacked. Calvert will not have a fun time in prison, no matter how strong he is."

Rose and her friends were at a separate table exchanging stories. Pete sat at her left and put his hand on her back gently. She didn't shake it off. Between the cheese and ice-cream courses, Pete gave her a present—a picture he had taken of a door in St. Pal. She kissed him and put her head on his shoulder.

De la Foi looked at them with a slight smile. "The sad part about aging is that your wisdom lags behind your age," he said. "I know exactly now what I should have done at 25. I recognize my duty and am proud to exercise it, but there is so much I have missed. So much."

"You did just save the planet, Christien," I reminded him, my hand on his arm.

Nuth came to visit us in New York shortly after our return from France. "What are you going to do with your money, Dr. Ecco?"

Ecco handed him a check. "Give it back to you of course," he said. "It's yours."

"No," said Nuth. "Dispose of it as you wish. The less money I have, the less I'll be tempted to reengage in politics."

Nuth could not be otherwise persuaded.

Ecco put some part of the money in the twins' names for college and sent almost all the rest to refugee aid in Darfur. With the little left over he offered to take Kate and me to Il Molino. The restaurant asked if he had a reservation.

"Well no, but I'm the well-known Dr. Ecco," he replied with assurance.

"Sorry?" the young voice responded. "We don't need a doctor right now."

"No, Dr. Ecco the mathematical detective," said Ecco. "You know the Ohio election fraud, the Warriors of the Rapture..."

"Sorry sir, but you need to make a reservation just like everyone else," we heard.

Ecco hung up and smiled. "My 15 minutes of fame have come and gone. That's mostly good, well, I guess. Anyone for Asian fusion food at Peep?"

Index